A Call To Connection

How to Connect to Self, Source, Spirit, Nature and Others

Frannie Rose Goldstein

Copyright © 2014 Frannie Rose Goldstein
All rights reserved.

ISBN: 1500537322
ISBN 13: 9781500537326

Dedication

For my beloved mother, Ethel Battalen Goldstein, who wanted me to have a life, and for my son, Auren Kaplan, who is my life.

Table of Contents

Acknowledgments — ix

All the World's a Stage... — xii
Prologue — xiii
The glorious sun... — xviii
Connecting To Source — 1
    Exercise for Connecting to the Light — 1
    Exercise For Reducing Have Tos — 6
Go to your bosom, knock there... — 8
Seeing With the Heart — 9
What is it she does now? Look how she rubs her hands... — 12
Clearing Negative Energy — 13
    Set Your Intentions with Gratitude — 14
    Hand washing — 14
    Epsom Salts Baths — 15
    Aromatherapy — 15
    Flower Essences — 16
    Smudging — 16
    Lighting Candles — 17
    Body Work — 17
    Spiritual Work — 19
    Reiki — 19
    Shamanic Merging and Journeying — 20
    The basic technique for the classic shamanic journey — 22
    Cuzco Clearing Technique — 22
    Cosmic Cookie Clearing Technique — 23
    Meditation — 23

Dig a Hole	24
Lay on the Earth	24
Clearing With Fire	24
Sweat Lodge (round like a bubble!)	25
O Wonder!...	30
Are We In Relationship?	31
True it is that we have seen better days...	36
My Bubbles Manifest	37
Sweet are the uses of adversity...	48
Connecting to Nature	49
Exercise for Earth Awareness:	51
Exercise to locate your power Spot:	51
Canst thou not minister to a mind diseas'd...	54
Medical Disconnection	55
Connecting To Life Force	57
Exercise for hugging a tree	58
Some pigeons, Davy, a couple of short-legged hens, a joint of mutton...	62
Food Culture and Life Force	63
Exercise to breathe Fully:	65
Sometime we see a cloud that's dragonish...	68
Synchronicity and Prayer by Decree	69
What a piece of work is man, how noble in reason,	
how infinite in facilities; in form...	72
The Human Condition	73
O day and night, but this is wondrous strange!...	76
Power Animals	77
There is special providence in the fall of a sparrow. If it be now, 'tis not to...	84
Rituals	85
Exercise To Transform a Negative Pattern through Ritual:	87
O That this too too solid flesh would melt....	90
Ups and Downs	91
Now, my co-mates and brothers in exile...	96

The Sacred Circle	97
At length her grace rose, and with modest paces...	102
Altars	103
If I profane with my unworthiest hand...	106
Touch Barriers	107
The Woosel cock so black of hue...	110
Natural Talents	111
Tomorrow, and tomorrow, and tomorrow...	116
Disappointment	117
Exercise for Shifting Disappointment Energy/ Automatic Writing	119
Like as the waves make towards the pebbled shore...	122
Time	123
Exercise for Clarity:	125
No more be done...	128
Death	129
Our revels now are ended. These our actors...	136
Caveat	137
Epilogue	139
End Notes	141
Bibliography	143
About the Author	147

Acknowledgments

Writing is a complicated process which involves so much more than coming up with words. Critical to this process are the input and suggestions from readers of the drafts. I want to thank Karen Bango for her objective encouragement and reminders that I have good things to say in a good way. Without her, this book would never have reached completion. Thanks to Lisa Gutowski, who said, "This one is for the masses", which I kept replaying in my head during all the days I was sure this one stunk. Also, Lisa tried many of the exercises and reported back quite positively about their effects. I am grateful to Sandra Ingerman, who was critical and encouraging at the same time, and who admonished me to "Make the words your own". A hearty thank you to Damaris Casado. Her fabulous Engineer's brain helped me pull the pieces together.

I also owe a debt of gratitude to past clients, students, and actors whose work with me informed these pages.

I appreciate and am grateful to my OR teachers: Beth Davis (Vision Quest); Brant Secunda (Dance of the Deer Foundation); Deborah Richardson (Method Acting); Durrette Lauckern (Reiki); Larry Peters (Tibetan Shamanism); Betsy Bergstrom (Shamanic Depossession); Lynette Knauss for my love of poetry; Martin de Maat (Improvisation); Myron Eshowsky (Peacemaking); Paula Brown, in whose French class I first discovered the concept of *authenticity*; Roberto Pomo (Directing); Sandra Ingerman (Soul Retrieval, Healing With Light); The Bear Tribe; Wind Daughter and Diane Duggan (Stonewater) my sweat lodge teachers.

I honor and thank my NOR power animal whose idea this was in the first place: *Kauyumari*. Thanks also to Elephant, Tiger, Lion,

Buffalo, Bear, Coyote, Eagle, Owl, and Red Tail Hawk. And in human form, my love and gratitude to my NOR teachers: Beta Star, Isis, Neva, Shulamite, Hiram…and Janus. Thank you. It took a village.

JAQUES:
All the world's a stage,
And all the men and women merely players,
They have their exits and entrances,
And one man in his time plays many parts,
His acts being seven ages. At first the infant,
Mewling and puking in the nurse's arms.
Then, the whining schoolboy with his satchel
And shining morning face, creeping like snail
Unwillingly to school. And then the lover,
Sighing like furnace, with a woeful ballad
Made to his mistress' eyebrow. Then a soldier,
Full of strange oaths, and bearded like the pard,
Jealous in honour, sudden, and quick in quarrel,
Seeking the bubble reputation
Even in the cannon's mouth. And then the justice
In fair round belly, with good capon lin'd,
With eyes severe, and beard of formal cut,
Full of wise saws, and modern instances,
And so he plays his part. The sixth age shifts
Into the lean and slipper'd pantaloon,
With spectacles on nose, and pouch on side,
His youthful hose well sav'd, a world too wide,
For his shrunk shank, and his big manly voice,
Turning again towards childish treble, pipes
And whistles in his sound. Last scene of all,
That ends this strange eventful history,
Is second childishness and mere oblivion,
Sans teeth, sans eyes, sans taste, sans everything.
    AS YOU LIKE IT, Act 2, Scene 7

Prologue

This is a book about connections; needing them, seeking them, finding them….Strengthening, expanding and, ultimately sharing them. Like delicate fibers of precious silk, we send out little trailers of our energy. What are we seeking? And where do they go? And, more importantly, what is it that happens when our tendrils of potentialities connect up with those of someone else?

Together in these pages we will explore our humanity, what propels us ever forward in search of one another, in search of a twin soul, a similar being who is somewhat LIKE US…who can validate and appreciate and applaud our very essence. For it is when we feel appreciated that we can expand our souls, and truly experience our shining authenticity.

It sounds wonderful…human beings seeking each other out like little heat missiles in the night… But where does all this start?

It starts with an idea…the little thought that rumbles around inside that says, "I live in this world with all these millions and millions of people. Some are like me, but most are not…how can I find my people?" This book attempts to show and share how you too can find the life organization, and potential for personal healing and growth, as you connect first to yourself, to Source, to Spirit, to Nature, and ultimately to others. From novice spiritual seeker to seasoned healer, there is something to connect with in A Call To Connection for each of us.

Imagine a room full of bubbles, Lawrence Welk style. Each is perfect in its way, dressed in glorious colors and swirling patterns. Each bubble is unique. Sometimes, you can see them piggybacking, one on top of the other. But have you ever looked closely at a bubble, under the bright light of a lamp, or the sun? Hold that bubble out there on your magic wand, and watch it closely. The colors meld and twirl and expand and contract and it's all very beautiful, magical really; but eventually, even when the "bubble reputation" is shining in your life, black dots start to enter the surface of the bubble, and the dots grow and mutate until they have overtaken the colorful light and finally, inevitably, the bubble bursts.

What do we do next? We blow yet another bubble, seeking clarity, color and connection to beauty all over again, even though we know before we even start, that after the beauty, come the black dots. This is life.

What keeps us going? What motivates us to "blow yet another bubble" despite the certainty that it will burst, in the end? It is the desire to live a self-actualized life, fulfilled to our greatest potentials, to be, before we are "not to be".

In every moment, we are each of us seeking something. None of us wants to be the only bubble left in the bottle. Most of us want to merge with other bubbles and celebrate together in a swirling dance of color and light. We want to reach out, to connect with others, to share in the dance, and appreciate the beauty of life together.

Our human species is comprised of social creatures. We live in community; we hunt in packs, and dish gossip over the campfires at twilight. We sing up the sun and murmur to the moon, and we tend to do these things with other individuals. When enough individuals merge with each other and celebrate in this dance of swirling color and light, we are capable of shifting the very essence of the energy both in and around us in miraculous ways. Everyone likes a good miracle. We just have forgotten how to believe in them. My intention is to show you that miracles are everywhere: just open your heart and eyes and ears and look and listen.

When I was growing up in the 50s and 60s, the clan groups were pretty clear. They were political or religious groups. There were also ethnic groups each bearing societal expectations around marriage, family and, career options; we knew we had a place, even if we didn't like it much, and even if we frankly wanted to flee the group. We knew going in that there was this room full of bubbles that already had a wand out for us. During the upheaval of the Vietnam era, our social systems began to swirl, like real bubbles, and little cancer dots eventually began to erode the status quo. Authority was questioned, and spiritual journeys were initiated. People tuned in and turned on and dropped out. Psychoactive substances altered our perceptions. On closer inspection, many of us began to feel that the original groups weren't always meeting our needs. We began to look at ourselves, and our communities and our groups in new and perhaps unorthodox ways, embracing Eastern religions, or aboriginal value systems.

Many of us noticed the myriad possibilities of the spiritual groups, the overlapping requirements of various religions, and the life altering shift in our mobility. The sheer magnitude of choices for where to plop down and hang our curtains became overwhelming to the point that many people just tuned out, and turned off, leading to national apathy on many levels.

Ironically, while many of us were bemoaning the lost connections of the "good old days", others among us were embracing new methodologies towards social connection and towards enlightenment. My personal passage took me from training to act, direct and produce plays, to achieving teacher certification, and ultimately training as a shamanic practitioner. As I moved one step at a time, whether tired or not, I moved closer and closer to being my own beautiful bottle of light, manifested in the glorious swirl that is the famous childhood "soap bubble" on a magic wand. This book intends to provide inspiration for others to find their way to a closer connection to self, source, spirit, nature and others. Whatever that way is! It can be used as a template for those of us who have aged into the New Age, as well as those who come behind us. As a shamanic practitioner, the ways of the non-ordinary spirit worlds necessarily color and light up my ordinary reality world.

A shamanic practitioner lives harmoniously in the natural world. Her task is to act as an intermediary between the realms, and become learned in the way to shift consciousness into Non-Ordinary Reality (NOR) to meet with her benevolent power animals and spiritual teachers to obtain information which can be returned to Ordinary Reality for the purpose of betterment of life, and self-actualization. Because I work with the light, I know I am of the light. This gives me the ability to truly live, in the deepest sense.

Then or now, the human instinct remains the same: we want to be a part of something, we want to dance the bubble dance in a riot of color and light, and we want to do it NOW, right away, FAST, before the black dots invariably cause the whole lovely, fragile display to burst and cease to exist.

We yearn to be connected to ourselves, our inner desires, our children, our parents, our work, our spirituality, our sexuality, our hearts, our minds….

It is through being connected to other human beings that our humanity comes most fully alive. And then we most enjoy the dance.

The glorious sun
Stays in his course and plays the alchemist
Turning with splendor of his precious eye
The meager cloddy earth to glittering gold.
                    SONNET

ROMEO:
But soft, what light through yonder window breaks?
It is the east, and Juliet is the sun.
                    ROMEO AND JULIET Act 2, scene 2

Connecting To Source

Life can be quite lonely when we're alone. Although Romeo and Juliet were forbidden to be together, their need to bond with a like-minded person was the strong motivating pull that cut through the prohibitions, even on pain of death. The sheltered teen aged Juliet was the sun, Romeo came to her in moonlight and colored her world with bubbles of love and desire. I have myself spent many hours moaning about how lonely I am, shy to go out and insinuate myself among other people. Oddly, for an outgoing woman, I can be very reticent about introducing myself to groups of unknown people. If Romeo was Juliet's entre to adult love, to find the strength to find my own band of bubbles, I had to learn how to plug in first.

Before we can connect to others, we must connect to ourselves, and we must connect to the Light Source from which our self is created. The glorious sun, Creator, God, All That Is, Great Spirit, Wankantanka, Buddha Energy, Christ Consciousness…the wellspring of all that is of the Light. We must first recognize that, in fact, we are already connected—and deeply—to that which made us in the first place. So we must find the first ray of our essence, and explore and embrace the totality of that initiative breath of life.

Exercise For Connecting to the Light:

Some may experience this as expansive and others may find it grounding. Your experience with this will be perfect for you. You might put on some relaxing instrumental music in the background. The scent of lavender oil or incense can be a gentle yet powerful addition. Close your eyes and invite peaceful relaxation. Allow yourself to breathe gently and slowly in through your nose, and out through your mouth. Ask for your energy to slow, to quiet down. Imagine you are breathing through your heart and allow your heart energy to flow. Ask for the first light ray of your life essence to be revealed to you at this moment. You may notice this at first as a small light in your heart. It may appear as a flame, or a sun, or a beam. You may have an experience of just knowing it is there. However it appears is perfect. Now you must give this light all of your attention. Ask this light to expand. Visualize the light filling your heart, and then the rest of your body, slowly reaching every corner, nook and cranny of yourself. As this light fills you, begin to hum, or tone or chant. With each voiced exhale, feel yourself connecting deeply to this initiative breath of life. This is not a memory. You are actually tapping back in to the original source of your being. Allow this breath of light/life to enfold you in a loving embrace. Breathe into the sound and the light for as long as you wish. This is you. This is what you are hoping someone will see, and connect with…someone does. The Source of All That Is, that birthed you, sees you. Let the feeling of deep connection surround and permeate your innermost secret places, real or imagined. And just be. Be connected.

It is important that we respect where it is that we are at any given moment in time. To know this, we must know where our heart is. Because that's where we are isn't it? Take a moment to look back at the Shakespeare quote for the Prologue. These famous lines, beginning with "All the world is a stage," remind us that "one man in his time plays many parts." This is the classic example of the passage of one man's life. It highlights the stages we must pass through on our way from infancy to the grave; from childhood, to adulthood, to respectability, to aging and losing our mentation and the childlike dependency of senility. We have but an allotted time on earth. So much of this precious and limited time, people are so busy doing, taking on added responsibilities when the most important ones are sometimes neglected. What do you think the most important connection in your life is? To your children, maybe? To your spouse or parents? Perhaps, but I believe that the single most important connection in your life is the one wherein you find your truest self. Your breath of life. No matter how the "have tos" pile up on your list, no matter the demands of home, job, client, family, you cannot be what you are not, and you cannot do what cannot be done. And you cannot be and you cannot do if you are separated from the source of your life breath, your inner bubble; your ray of the 'Creator Light'.

This sounds so simple, and it is; yet we live complicated lives, with layers of complexities, and duties, and "have tos". With all that energy riffling around us, how are we supposed to respect where we are, or even know where we are?

Life is funny. When we forget to stop and honor where we are (busily focused on where we think we should be), things happen, sometimes unpleasant things, that propel us right out of our "have tos" and into the immediacy of the *now*.

The spring my son was a senior in high school, I was working myself into quite a state of "have to". I had a long list of "essential" things to accomplish, and I'd given myself one month. I had to go on two college trips with my son and his father from whom I'd been long divorced. It was a challenging collision of my past and present. I had to address the graduation announcements and sort photos, plus plan and implement a graduation party. My home is modest, so an outdoor party would necessitate ordering tents, tables and chairs. I had to attend my niece's college graduation in a different state. I had to be at work and I had responsibilities to my students and clients. I had to see that the new sweat lodge was built, already long overdue, and schedule a community lodge. I had to ready the garden, move the firewood, clean the patio, mow the lawn, continue my spiritual work, check in on my aging parents, figure out how to survive after the child support ended…phew, and the "have to" list was actually longer than this. I felt consequently burdened and stressed. The more I piled on myself to do, and the more I had to do alone, the more overwhelmed I became.

But where was I through all of this? Where was my light-self, my breath of life? Not flowing. I felt stressed, agitated, beating the clock, and frustrated.

Here comes the funny part. On a college visit to Georgetown University, I stayed with an old friend to save money on the hotel. He and his fiancé had recently bought a stately older home in a lovely spot in the city. Enjoying the early spring, I paraded around their home in happy but chilly bare feet, enjoying their Jacuzzi bath tub and the flowering trees all around me. Then I donned a pair of socks to warm my feet, but coming down off the staircase I slipped on the lovely hard wood floor. I went into a full skid, like a ball player slamming into home plate, barreling into an inordinately high marble threshold. Wham! And life changed in a moment. Injury, pain, immobility, the denial of gardening and activity, plus a long process of diagnosis through trial and error, found me one month later, sitting and whining and moping and hurting. Okay, maybe not so funny, but the truth was, *that's where I was at.* And none of that other "have to" stuff was getting done. My focus was on trying to get my foot to heal. *And that's where my energy was.* Slowly I began to realize I could not even start to accomplish the "have tos". The list rapidly shrank to mostly medical appointments, and my activities became limited to those around my son's last month in high school.

The new sweat lodge did not get constructed for several months, the party did not get planned, and my aging mother came over to try to help me out instead. Accepting and embracing where I was—homebound—was a great challenge. As an active person, the forced inaction was quite frustrating. I kept trying to change what was happening, to will the pain away, and somehow speed up the healing process. I gave myself a daily Reiki treatment, wonderful healing energy that I had studied for many years. I asked friends to pray for me and send healing energy and light. I tried to stay connected to the light, and to the sound of the breath of life. I understood I had to do more with all this sitting time than complain despite how tempting that was. (Self-pity is also part of the human condition; but it's clearly not terribly helpful).

Sometimes our "have tos" are so compelling, they can steal our center. The problem is that the more circumstances pull us away from center, the more the darkness will find a place to abide. *When we are not fully living as we are, we become more and more in conflict. Conflict constricts the energy flow, pain expands and shadows move in. Suffering ensues.*

The Reiki self-sessions helped to bring me to center. After seven days of consecutive Reiki treatments on myself, I felt balanced enough to journey to visit my spiritual allies for information, healing, help and hope. Here I want to return briefly to the topic of shamanic journeying. There will be many references, and much more detail to come; however, for our present purpose, let me sum it up once again: A shamanic journey is one in which a person shifts their consciousness from the world of ordinary reality where we spend our lives into the world of non-ordinary reality usually with the sonic drumming sound, or rattle in the background. This is done to retrieve positive information from benevolent power animals and spiritual teachers and other allies. For now, I want to share that one of the most magical elements of the shamanic journey is the element of surprise, and during my journey I encountered a doozy of a surprise!

"Write a book," I was told, by Kauyumari (Deer), "And the pain will go away." Huh?

Although somewhat startled by this, I literally moved from journey state to the computer, and this endeavor was seeded in that moment. To utilize this life moment of forced immobility as an opportunity for creative self- expression made sense on multiple levels. It gave shape and meaning to my personal angst. Frequently we miss the gifts we've prayed for, because they come in unusual disguises sometimes. Throughout the course of my son's senior year of high school the nagging question had long been, "What's next for me?" As usual, the spirits have their own ideas about what it is we mere mortals should be doing for the betterment of all parties. I had just been given a fat clue.

I had asked what I was to write about. And I was told to write about "being connected". As I see it, this means being connected to light source, and to life breath. Moreover, this means being willing to learn how to take care of myself in a variety of methods that I can connect to and enact all by myself! This takes willingness, and time, and attention. How do we stay connected to the source, when our bodies are wracked with pain, or our teenagers are shouting in our face, or the bills are piling up, or your lover has herpes, or your parents are fighting and you just feel overwhelmed? I have learned from listening to my clients, predominantly middle aged people, that most folks are yearning for simple techniques to calm their lives, spark their potentials, relax, and feel fully whole. With intention, I hope to share here many simple methods I have either learned over the years, or developed on my own to become useful to enable the busy adult to find the space to quiet and turn in to the light.

First we must slow down. If we can voluntarily turn our "have tos" into "want tos", so much the better. It is important that we only commit to what is reasonable. Contrary to a lot of modern magazines, we are not super beings that can do it all; nor should we be. If we're not sure where we are, or *are* sure that where we are is *not* where we want to be, then we need to stop. Just. Stop.

Breathe. Turn on the life breath. Turn on the source light. Connect to the initial ray of light. Connect to the first sound of breath. And just be.

Exercise For Reducing Have Tos:

For you list makers, this will be fun. First, without censorship or editing of any kind, make a list of all the things you feel you have to accomplish at this moment in your life. It can be as long as you like. Now, go back down the list, and next to each item, write down what you think is likely to happen if the item isn't accomplished. Did you include staying connected to the light on your list? Now, go back down the list one more time asking yourself the question, "Does this serve my energy right now?" It is very easy for us to get caught up in the "shoulds" of life; my experience has taught me that genuine "shoulds" take care of themselves. It is easy to spend a lot of time chasing after activities that not only don't serve the energy of where we are at the moment, but, in fact, may actually undermine where we need to be. Whatever path the reader chooses, it is good to follow it in a disciplined manner. This way one takes a bit of time each day to connect to Source, which enables not only the connection to Source, but the resulting inner courage to follow through per the guidance received.

Staying centered in the light makes it easier to distinguish between what is essential and what is not. My heart has fully embraced the sentiment Antoine de Saint Exupery expressed in his tender book, "The Little Prince": "It is only with the heart that one can see rightly. What is essential, is invisible to the eye".

*Go to your bosom, knock there,
and ask your heart what it doth know.*
　　　　　　　MEASURE FOR MEASURE

Seeing With the Heart

Do you ever just know something? In your heart, in your core, you just know it to be true? Think for a moment of a time you felt that way. Sit with that feeling for a few moments until you can easily recall what it feels like, and how it feels in your body. That is what it feels like, to see with an open heart. Some people call it intuition. Some people call it clarity or love. Whatever you call it, life works most smoothly when you honor this inner knowing, and give life to these inner truths through your energy and attention.

Of course, people around you are quite fond of trying to undo your faith in your knowing. Families and friends, while well meaning, are frequently very adept at undermining our belief in ourselves. I recommend that when you have something you know to be true in your heart, sit with that knowing for a time until it is strong enough to withstand peer review! It comes down to whether or not you trust yourself. I have found that frequently people who are beginning a spiritual journey have more obstacles in this area than anything else. When I went for Vision Quest with the Bear Tribe in 1991, my teacher Beth Davis cautioned against too much conversation following the three days alone on the mountain. She counseled sitting with the experience for 24 hours to let it gel before giving it away in speech. I heeded this advice, and when I finally did give voice to my experiences I achieved a real epiphany, and made spiritual connections that only happened because I had let them gestate. Sun Bear, the Ojibwa medicine man who founded the Bear Tribe, was the visionary who brought the medicine wheel gatherings back to this continent. He used to say, "In gentleness there is great strength. Power most of the time can be a very quiet thing."

When I work with soul retrieval clients, trust issues frequently emerge as a preliminary obstacle. Spirit led rituals can often ameliorate trust issues. Shamanism is rich with opportunities to receive spirit led rituals that can specifically target an individual's need not only to see in their heart and hear their inner truth, but to proactively take steps which strengthen their ability to believe in themselves, fully, and once and for all. Ritual gleaned from shamanic journey can often be surprisingly fun! The spirits have great humor. Immensely powerful healings can result from rituals that seem silly or funny when enacted with intention and attention. I once brought back a ritual for a woman which required her to twirl a daisy in her fingers every day for a period of time, along with some other instructions. She was delighted! She said that daisies were her favorite flower and she was looking forward to filling her house with them. She later reported great success as a result of her performing the spirit given ritual.

Once we are clear where our hearts are and fill our days with connection to our Source we will still experience challenges at times due to the obstacles that life presents. We may discover the way, but realize it may be fraught with peril. Thus it becomes essential that we can navigate these rough waters without straying too far from source and center. The next chapter will offer concrete tools to facilitate being centered and having peace of mind.

DOCTOR:
What is it she does now? Look how she rubs her hands.

GENTLEWOMAN:
It is an accustom'd action with her, to seem thus
Washing her hands. I have known her continue in this a quarter of
An hour.

LADY MACBETH:
Yet here's a spot.

DOCTOR:
Hark, she speaks. I will set down what comes from her, to
satisfy my remembrance the more strongly.

LADY MACBETH:
Out, damn'd spot! Out, I say!—One; two: why, then
'tis time to do't.—Hell is murky.—Fie, my lord, fie, a soldier, and
afeard? What need we fear who knows it, when none can call our
pow'r to accompt?—Yet who would have thought the old man to
have had so much blood in him?

MACBETH Act 5, scene 1

Clearing Negative Energy

In the preceding Shakespeare passage from "The Tragedy of Macbeth", we see the doctor and Macbeth negotiating for his wife's sanity. The doctor's counsel: Lady Macbeth needs to turn inward to discover the source of her terrible pain. Lady Macbeth is never able to reconcile the vile act of murder, and plunges into a morass of sleep walking, reliving the dastardly deed she shares with her husband, and ultimately, dies from guilt. Dark times for Lady M.

Dark times for all of us. This book can help. Contained herein are many opportunities for the Readers to discover or refresh systems they can employ that will smooth out the rough edges of their busy outer and busier inner lives. The bubble is beautiful, but those black cancer dots are coming. What to do?

Negative or dark energy exists. It is the flip side of light. One cannot exist without its counterpart. While you are seeing with your heart, you may also see the darkness in its variety of forms: illness, stress, accidents, anger, spiritual possessions, intrusions, bad moods, scary dreams…and so on. It is good to acknowledge the dark forces so that they don't need to come looking for you. It is also important to keep the darkness at bay.

Negative energy can take multiple forms and reach you in myriad ways. Its purpose is singular: to interfere with your connection to the Light. Think of it as psychic detritus, the amorphous and unfocused negative energy emitted by people around us, frequently strangers. Bad tempers, foul moods, insults, curses, the "evil eye", hostile drivers, road rage, check-out line temper tantrums…this is the fodder for "psychic detritus". These kinds of thoughts and energy forms are floating around our beautiful bubbles, popping them prematurely and causing distress in our lives. It is important to periodically and regularly cleanse yourself of this mantle that gloms onto you at will and without permission. Otherwise, you will fill up with other people's negative energy which will foul your ability to remain centered and healthy.

The good news is many options abound for dispelling negativity from the simple techniques to the more complex. For large negative energies, such as intrusions and possessions, it is best to seek out the assistance of a qualified intermediary. Shamanic healing can be instrumental in this. There can be present a kind of intrusion that wreaks havoc in an individual; this is much more commonly observed than previously considered by the general population. For the more common types of negative energy we take on in our daily lives, a variety of techniques are available to clear them. What follows are some simple suggestions, though this is by no means a finite list. I encourage experimentation with aromatherapy, and rituals, and of course journeys. For those of you who have a shamanic practice, I recommend journeying for specific rituals to assist with clearing negative energy, in addition to these techniques:

- *Set Your Intentions With Gratitude*

Every morning after I've filled the bird feeders, I give thanks for all that is working or that I'd like to see working in my life. I have embraced the ritual of setting my intention to go safely and smoothly through the day. I also call for peace to be within me and without as well as calling for peace on earth now. I call for all sentient and suffering beings to be at peace. In this way I send energy to all who need help, and in my small way I contribute to the swirl of positive energy on the planet. Although it can be a struggle to maintain the peacefulness all day, at least I start with a calm and balanced demeanor and spirit. You can "reset" your intentions throughout the day if necessary.

- *Hand Washing*

The washing of hands is an easy, simple way to shift from one energetic mode to another. Quick help can be achieved with old fashioned soap and water. Lava soap is especially useful for this purpose, but not required. After returning home from work or errands, a focused hand washing can make a lot of difference in how you approach the rest of your day. The trick is to do it three times one right after the other. Visualize the stress washing away. I usually take a moment to breathe deeply and allow the fresh, clean feeling to permeate my entire energy field and inner consciousness.

- Epsom Salts Baths

This is fabulous. Epsom salts have long been a traditional home remedy for sore feet, or pink eye, and now it is available for energetic clearing. The recipe is to take a quart of Epsom salts per hot bath, soak, and relax as long as you can; however, make sure the water stays hot while you're in it to prevent the salts from releasing the negativity hey have absorbed back into the cooler water. When you are finished you'll find this refreshing and very soothing. Epsom salts are not to be confused with mineral salt baths, and the resulting feeling is different. Mineral salts leave me relaxed and calm; Epsom salts leave me feeling energized and clear.

- *Aromatherapy*

A simple and refreshing method for lifting a negative mental state is to use lavender oil or other scents for aromatherapy. You can add a few drops to a bath, or to a light bulb ring, or use as incense. Despite the warning that says to use it on your skin only in carrier oil, I have successfully applied pure lavender directly to my face, around my nostrils and throat for a quick fix. Other useful oils I've encountered are rosemary, and citrus. Ylang Ylang, Neroli and Patchouli are other calming aromas. Rosemary applied to the back of the neck is especially useful for preventing unwanted intrusive energy from attaching itself to us. Go lightly with Rosemary, excessive and prolonged neck application can leave your neck feeling numb. For relief, just stop the Rosemary oil for a few days, and cut back on the amount. Less is more. For people who work in hospitals and nursing homes, it is definitely indicated! Feel free to experiment with different scents as you discover what works best for you.

- *Flower Essences*

I am a firm believer in the healing power of flower essences. Readily available at most health food stores, they cost about $12 a bottle. The Bach company puts out a pamphlet that lists the available essences, and describes which best apply to a wide variety of mood or mental states. Many of you may be familiar with the popular Bach Rescue Remedy tincture or cream, but it is good to become familiar with the variety they have to offer. Gentle, safe, over the counter, and impossible to overdose means you can have confidence in their usage. Some of my favorites are White Chestnut for persistent and unwanted thoughts; Sweet Chestnut for despondency, Elm when you feel overwhelmed by responsibilities, and Walnut for life transitions. These are but a few. I hope you'll discover the beneficial, healing and centering properties that come to us from the flower family. Additionally, you can make your own special essences, of up to 6 different Bach remedies!

- *Smudging*

I will always cherish the memory of the first time I was fanned with the smoke of burning sage. "Smudging" or burning sage, sweet grass, cedar or juniper can lift the energy around one's auric body, and dispel negative energies from a room. Sage takes away the darkness; sweet grass brings in the light. Cedar honors all that give away in support of your healing. For safety, and also traditionally, it is good to use a large abalone shell or other heat resistant container. Place a small handful of the dried plant into the container. Light it with a match, then blow out the flames letting it smoke a bit. With your hands or a feather, fan the smoke to get a good burn, then draw the smoke to your heart, head and around your entire body. I like to waft the smoke down the front of my body and up the back of my body. This follows a natural flow of energy. You can play around with the flow by fanning the smoke in the reverse directions and see how that makes you feel. Remember that fanning downward is more grounding, fanning upward is uplifting, and our needs for the direction of the smoke may change per situation.

- *Lighting Candles*

If you can do this safely, buy some slow burning (usually 7 day) white candles, usually found in religious stores, and sometimes in grocery stores. With a pen or unfolded paper clip, scratch the words of a *positive* intention onto the surface of the candle. As the candle burns, the intentions are activated. I have frequently incorporated this technique when holding community sweat lodges. I would scratch my intention for safe travel for all participants as well as for love, and healing, and cleansing. With that candle glow shining, I felt I had blanketed the participants with etheric protection. Long after the ceremony concluded, and the people had driven home, the light continued to offer the blessings I had inscribed.

In general, candles are most useful for lighting up dark corners in the house. According to the principles of *Feng Shui*, this will bring more light into your life. Of course, whenever burning candles it is imperative to do so safely. When burning 7 day candles, I usually keep them on a high mantle where the cats cannot get to them. Shower ledges are another safe place, though watch out in case you drop the glass!

- *Body Work*

There are many types of body work that you can utilize to dissipate the rigors of physical or emotional stress. Body work fosters a sense of relaxation and wellbeing. In this regard *yoga* is unsurpassed. Along with the physical benefits yoga provides, it speaks to a person's emotional and spiritual states as well. Regular yoga practice provides for "the health and beauty of the organism as a unified whole. Weight control, slimming, firming, relief of tension and stiffness, improvement in general health, emergence of hidden beauty, emotional stability and a positive outlook" (Hittelman 8). There are different yoga styles to meet individual needs and classes seem to be plentiful nowadays. Check your local community for classes which are offered by hospitals as part of their complementary medicine programs, too. If you prefer a solitary practice as I do, Richard Hittelman's book <u>Yoga 28 Day Exercise Plan</u>, offers practical, easy to follow, step by step instructions complete with useful photos and inspiring commentary. As with any recommendation in this book, be sure to find a teacher who inspires you and with whom you feel comfortable and safe. You are never required to stay with a teacher you don't like!

Regular or even occasional *therapeutic massage* also provides for deep healing and relaxation. As with yoga, there are many kinds of massage including Swedish massage, Shiatsu, Neuro-Muscular massage, and more. These days massage therapists are combining other alternative healing modalities into their work as well. Many import and health food stores sell a variety of modern self-massagers including reflexology root rollers; however, 45 minutes of an attentive full body massage with a skilled massage therapist can soothe and replenish the body and spirit in a more profound way. Many cities have massage schools which offer reduced rate massages by their students. There is a fine school in my area, Irene's Myomassology Institute where the students do a very fine job at reduced rates.

Kum Nye relaxation is a system of movement exercises and self- massage that you can practice alone. A healing system that gently alleviates stress, Kum Nye assists in our achieving enjoyment and finding gratitude in daily living. It transforms negative habits thus helping us to become centered and healthy. We become content, our senses and hearts open to joy (Tulku, viii).

There is no shortage of life trauma and stress which can cause physical harm to our bodies. The fact that many people reflect their inner tension in their outer body is no secret anymore. *Holistic physicians* have long held the view that it is essential to treat the patient as an individual comprised of body, mind, heart and spirit.

More than 25 million Americans, and millions more elsewhere have been the lucky recipients of *chiropractic care*. The chiropractic physician melds ancient healing philosophies with modern techniques. Chiropractors have learned that while we have the potential power to heal ourselves naturally, our ability to successfully do this is often compromised by spinal nerve stress. Through spinal manipulation and adjustments, this spinal nerve stress is alleviated thus making it more possible for us to feel well. Spinal adjustments reduce stress, increase resistance to illness and improve overall body function. Chiropractic care can also mean the difference between a life of health, strength and vitality or one of weakness and disability.

- *Spiritual Work*

When our energy is devitalized, we become even more susceptible to illness, trauma and psychic detritus. By spending practice time connecting to the pure light of the Creator (using the exercise we discussed earlier), you can literally feel your-self shifting from the density of negativity to the lightness of a cloud. There is a technique called *transfiguration*. The process of transfiguration itself is not complicated. The technique involves metaphorically releasing yourself as you know yourself. This process, done through guided visualization or shamanic journey is known as "dismemberment." Within this construct, you allow yourself to fall apart and ask to be put back together in a complete state of divinity. Through shifting your consciousness to connect with the light of all things, you allow this light to permeate your new being. Follow this by humming, or tone vocally to maintain the connection with the light. *The toning seems to be the catalyst for the duration of the connection* (Ingerman). When I first learned how to do this, there was a part of the exercise where we were sent out of doors to continue toning outside in nature. This was profound and exciting for me, as I felt I was hearing melodic responses from the trees. I wandered out onto the top of a hill, still toning, still blissed out. There I saw Karla, another workshop participant at the bottom of the hill. She grinned up at me and toned, and I grinned down at her and toned and we were completely in unison, completely wedded to the light. It was a thing of beauty I cannot fathom forgetting

- *Reiki*

Reiki is another wonderful tool for clearing negativity and promoting healing, wholeness and well-being. It uses protected symbols to unlock and connect with the universal healing light energy. Reiki is a gentle form of healing touch/non touch. Reiki can be easily taught so that you can treat yourself; additionally, a plethora of Reiki healers abound who can give you treatments. Of course, not all healers are created equal, and you are encouraged to ask around, get references, and be sure you have found someone with integrity and a loving nature to assist you, I feel this is crucial and try to bring this to my work. Reiki is unbeatable for getting centered and bringing in positive energy and supporting the healing process. It can be used in conjunction with allopathic medicines. It is so respected nowadays, in fact, that many complementary medicine programs for cancer patients routinely offer Reiki sessions in addition to traditional medical treatments. For myself, I have studied to reach the stage of what is called "Reiki Master"....despite my abilities to perform this healing, I continue to be uncomfortable with the title. I feel I am an eternal student, master of nothing, accomplishing what I can with the help of my allies. Indeed, I can get somewhat irritated when I hear, "Oh, I'm a Reiki Master", as it smacks of spiritual materialism, and seems to deny the very loving and giving aspect of this healing modality. This recalls when I heard Brant Secunda, notable shaman of the Huichol Indians who live in the Sangre De Cristo Mountains in Mexico, remark that if one says they are a shaman, they are not. That's kind of what happens to me when people announce, "I'm a Reiki Master".

- *Shamanic Merging and Journeying*

For those of us who practice shamanism, the technique of 'merging with our power animals' helps us to hold some of our positive energy, and bring us to center in the midst of adversity. The idea here, is that the shamanic practitioner enters NOR and invites her power animal or spiritual teacher to literally merge with her spirit and become one. The Tibetan shamans visualize the power animal on top of the head melting down into the body. You can also visualize your power animal in your abdomen, spreading throughout your body from that point. Whichever works is fine. One note: many times in this book I am referring to power animals, and I want to clarify that I am talking only about a benevolent spiritual helper that has been retrieved through proper shamanic technique, by a reputable shamanic practitioner, i.e., one who has a strong relationship with her own helping spirits. Many times clients will say, "Oh, my power animal is such and such" because they have an affinity with the particular animal, and not because this animal is actually their spiritual helper. Frequently, the animal retrieved for a client isn't anything expected. In any case, this merger between spirit and human is good for the spirit helper, as well, who can enjoy being present in ordinary reality for a time.

As always, we must remember to thank and honor these animals that protect us. I have even found that merging with my power animal has helped alleviate some of the stress of being stuck in traffic; particularly when the person behind me continues to bear down as if to plow right over me! By filling with power and expanding my field spiritually, I create a buffer between me and those that potentially can harm me. I have frequently utilized this merging technique, and more often than not, shortly afterwards the obnoxious driver either pulls into another lane, or eases off my tail. Check out the chapter in this book on Power Animals for more on my perspective.

I do want to clearly state that while shamanism is a central motif in my life, it is not the ultimate purpose of *this* book; which, rather, is to acquaint the novice or seasoned individual with a multiplicity of techniques to enrich their lives, and provide for a variety of healing and peace making techniques. Having said that, ancient shamanic wisdom can be a key part of the healing of one's essential spirit; additionally, it can powerfully assist in the emergence of one's authentic self and innate gifts meant to be manifested in this lifetime. When one's spirit is empowered, one's physical body is stronger. Shamanism is at least a 40,000 year old cross-cultural healing tradition in which the shamanic practitioner journeys into the spirit world outside of ordinary time and space to bring back knowledge and healing on behalf of a client (or pet, or piece of land, water, or building). Positive transformations often result when the shamanic practitioner uses ritual, drumming, singing and journeying to meet her power animals and teachers to learn hidden truths, retrieve power, retrieve essential soul parts, extract spiritual intrusions, or gain NOR assistance to resolve OR reality problems.

Shamanism is a complementary healing practice which does not interfere with allopathic medicines in general, and clients would continue with their medicines during and after healings, unless otherwise indicated by one's own physician. Truthfully, it is impossible to work together shamanically when the client is schizophrenic, and in this case psychiatric medications would need to be administered by a qualified psychiatrist, and your client stabilized before he would be able to reap any benefit from shamanic intervention. In this case, what's needed probably IS ordinary reality. Still, shamanic healing can be a great boost to psychotherapy, sometimes revealing in minutes what can take years to uncover in traditional therapy. I've often joked I'd love to get Woody Allen off the couch and onto the healing blanket aka the earth, a place where healings are often held.

- The basic technique for the classic shamanic journey:

You will want to utilize sonic (rythmic) drumming or rattling to the rhythm of 205-220 beats per minute (Harner 31). This can be accomplished with your own drum or rattle, or through a CD of sonic drumming or rattling. Allow yourself about 10 minutes for the first one. You set your intention beforehand. For example, for your first journey, you probably just want to get to your landscape in NOR, and explore it a bit before attempting to meet your power animal. With the assistance of the drumming sound, you will begin the journey by imagining you are entering a hole in the ground (figurative or literally remembered), which segues into a tunnel, and at the end of the tunnel you will see a light that opens up to your own personal shamanic landscape. It is here, in consult with your power animals, that you can obtain important and timely information. Said information can be visual or auditory, or present just as an inner knowing. When the rhythm of the drumming shifts from the fast regular beat to a different set of beats, this is the indication that it is time to conclude the journey. Saying thank you to all that came, return the same way you arrived, reversing your steps back through the tunnel, and out through the hole in the ground.

- *Cuzco Clearing Technique*

Shamanic, indigenous societies utilize powerful healing techniques, many of which can easily be adapted to our modern lifestyle. For example, there is a particularly simple and helpful clearing technique which stems from the Cuzco tradition. This is an interesting technique for dispensing negative energy that works especially well with negative mental states. The technique uses breath, light, and visualization. **How to do it:** Visualize a Pac-man like creature located in your abdomen. It looks like a big mouth. As you inhale, the Pac-man literally chews up the negative energy, and it is good to see this happen. As you exhale, visualize the chewed up crumbs of negativity leaving your body through your feet, and become absorbed into the earth. At the same time, the space emptied of the crumbs now fills with light. Continue this visualization and breathing process for several minutes until you feel cleared, released and peaceful. The beauty of this exercise is you can do it anywhere at any time without anyone noticing

- *Cosmic Cookie Clearing Technique*

This is fast and simple and very effective and can be used by yourself or for another. I fell in love with this technique because it is quick, can be done in public, and the positive results affected me immediately, as well as my partner when I first learned it. You position your hand as if it's holding a giant mall sized cookie and place it over the sacrum, but not touching. You voice your intention, that the positive healing energy of the universe should remove whatever negativity is ready to be removed at this time. After a few minutes pass you will feel a shift in your energy field, or notice the other person breathe differently, or sigh. This has immediate benefits, and has the advantage of being completely portable, all you need is you!

- *Meditation*

No discussion of self-healing techniques for vanquishing negativities would be complete without some commentary on the potential benefit that is achieved through meditation. In simple terms, meditation is an antidote to the clutter in our minds which can cause self-delusion, anxiety, and suffering. Meditation helps bring into balance the contrast between what we perceive something to be, and what actually is. Through simply paying attention to our breath and focusing on a mantra, we calmly sit, and breathe. Images and thoughts will surge in the mind, as they generally do. This time we will slow down, and notice them, one at a time. Through continued focus on breath and mantra, the images and thoughts will pass. Focus breath…new images. Focus breath…sit comfortably with a straight back…breathing in through the mouth and out through the nose…eyes slightly closed…feet on the ground…the mind calms, the thoughts flicker by like television images…breathing brings us back to what is.

- *Dig a Hole*

The challenge here is to find a place in nature where you will be able to let down your inhibitions. You will need a little tobacco for an offering, small trowel, corn kernel, a bean, and a squash seed. Dig a small hole, then for about an hour, speak into this hole saying whatever you need to say to release whatever it is that ails you directly into the hole. Give your tears and fears and pains directly to the earth Mother. When you have finished, plant your corn, bean and squash in the hole as a thank you, add a bit of tobacco so that your healing work will "grow corn".

- *Lay on the Earth*

This is easy, free, and requires no tools, techniques, methods or notebooks. Lie on your stomach, face downward and let your heart beat meld with that of the earth. Inhale the aromas of freshness. Let yourself feel the nurturance and support, the foundation for all your life. Enjoy it. Watch it bring you to back to center.

- *Clearing With Fire*

Fire is a great purifier that works in a variety of ways. Fire can carry our prayer requests to those that can answer, and Fire can also transmute negative energy. For many years while my son was growing up, the two of us celebrated the Winter Solstice with a Fire ceremony that we created at home. I share this only as one example of the myriad creative possibilities of self-generated ceremony. This can be adapted in any way that speaks to you. We did the ceremony indoors, but it would be wonderful outside, too. We began by smudging ourselves with sage to remove negative energies, and smudging our materials. These consisted of two large index cards, a metal mixing bowl (if doing the ceremony indoors and if, like ours, your gas fireplace precludes actually putting anything into it), tobacco, matches or lighter, pens, candles, and water). Lighting a candle is an important way to signal to the benevolent and helping spirits that you are calling to them.

Once we'd assembled our tools, we settled down on a rug in front of the fireplace, laying out the altar from the Pipe bundle. We each took a card, and on one side we wrote down everything we had encountered or engendered that year that no longer served us, which we wished to release from our lives. On the other side, we wrote down all the wonderful energies we wished to manifest in our lives for the coming year. After that, we shared a sacred Pipe ceremony, in which we prayed to release the old and unwanted, and to welcome the new. We also blessed the cards with smoke from the Pipe, the breath of our prayers made visible. We included a tobacco offering for our cards, which we placed in the metal bowl. The ashes from the Pipe stem were added in to the bowl, as well. At the end of the ceremony, we released our prayers for past and future by carefully burning the cards. Watching your negativities go up in flame is very evocative. The water was in case the fire escaped the bowl, which it never did. Because it is not a simple matter to acquire a Pipe, which I liken to a spiritual calling, you may need to omit this from the Fire ritual. If you have no access to one, This burning ritual becomes a simple ceremony which on its own can be quite empowering. Let the bubbles of intention stir the embers in your heart and breathe into the peace of connection. For our little mom and son family, we enjoyed a shared quiet and quality time together, a special bonding bonus.

Again, these are just a few ideas to get you started. There are all manner of options to work with herbs, feathers, stones, toning, chakras, auras and more. There is the ubiquitous sauna, and my own calling, the sweat lodge ceremony.

- *Sweat Lodge (round like a bubble!)*

As a trained Water Pourer (one who leads the sweat lodge ceremony), this is my particular favorite method for purging negativities and restoring self to a state of balance: mentally, emotionally, spiritually and physically. To bring forward a sweat lodge requires a big commitment of time and resources, both human and natural. Wood and stones are needed for the ceremonial fire. Water is poured during the ceremony. Honoring and healing herbs are also used. Blankets or other coverings placed over the lodge provide for the darkness inside. Done in four rounds, the sacred stones are heated in a ceremonial fire and are brought into the lodge pit during the ceremony. In the darkened lodge, participants sit close to the earth and experience the warmth of the womb of Mother Earth. The drum is used to align us to the heart beat of the Mother. Songs and chants call in the spirit helpers. The water is poured over the stones and the steam gently filters down like a warm embrace. In the safety of the Mother's arms, there is a freedom and awakening that is powerful and beautiful.

In my lodges, the goal is to nurture the people and create a safe and compassionate space for one's healing work both inside and outside the lodge itself. *The gifts of the sweat lodge will help one to purify and strengthen mentally, emotionally, physically and spiritually in order to assist in the creation and implementation of one's own visions.* They also give the healing, purpose and focus one requires to move forward in life in a good way. The cleansing is multifaceted. People have opportunities to deeply connect with and honor the elements, the four directions and the swimmers, crawlers, flyers, four and two legged beings, flowers, rivers... otherwise summed up as "all my relations." Participants can give voice to their dreams, giveaways, needs and prayers for themselves, their loved ones, communities, world leaders and Mother Earth. Inside the lodge, we sing and drum to honor the spirit keepers at different times during the ceremony. Everyone has an opportunity to join in and lend their voices and hearts to spirit. Usually there is a feast following the lodge, which is grounding, but also promotes connection to community and convivial fellowship.

The concept of healing through heat and sweat is age-old and world-wide. Most spiritual traditions incorporate some kind of healing with water and heat. Think of visiting hot springs, a Finnish sauna, or the Jewish Mikvah baths. In the United States, the sweat lodge comes to us from the example of our indigenous forebears, but even in the U.S. there are differences between the traditions. *In any case, it is important to* acknowledge the wisdom of the indigenous elders, and to be respectful when seeking assistance from their healing modalities. There are still those who believe that when white people use red people's healing techniques it is just another example of what has been stolen from them. Others feel that the gifts of healing come from the Creator and encourage this healing technique as a method for bridging differences between groups and promoting personal, communal and ecological healing. There may be some truth to both credos. The trick is to be respectful of the tradition practiced wherever you go to do a sweat lodge.

Additionally, as in many healing modalities, you may run into certain Water Pourers without proper training, or without proper respect for the sweat lodge traditions on this continent. As always, take the time to do some research and ask around so that you can find a reputable Water Pourer who operates from a place of love and light and who is well trained in the possible ramifications and effects of the totality of the experience. Powerful emotional and psychological breakthroughs can sometimes occur in the lodge. Also, intense heat is not recommended for everyone, particularly people with heart problems, blood pressure issues, those taking certain psychoactive drugs or those with fever or certain infectious diseases. The beautiful and powerful sweat lodge ceremony does need to be led by someone who is fully equipped to deal with any eventuality. Be sure you have a high level of comfort and safety, that you feel you have been prepared by the people in charge, and that you have been able to have your questions answered in advance. With these simple precautions, you will then go on to experience the cleansing and purifying and enlightening aspects in the most beneficial and therapeutic manner.

The sweat lodge is all about experiencing connections. It provides ample opportunity for participants to connect deeply with the elements, fire, air, water, earth. People can find pathways to their innermost needs, and can identify aspects of their life's journey with a particular clarity. Connecting with the spirits ultimately means connecting with your authenticity; and the connection with community while feasting and laughing afterward is equally potent. *If you want to change your direction, visualize your dreams, cleanse your body of toxins, sing in fellowship, touch the spiritual side of your nature, then the sweat lodge is the place for you and me.*

MIRANDA:
O wonder!
How many goodly creatures are there here!
How beauteous mankind is! O brave new world
That has such people in't!
                THE TEMPEST Act 5, scene 1

Let me not to the marriage of true minds
Admit impediments. Love is not love
Which alters when it alteration finds,
Or bends with the remover to remove.
O no, it is an ever-fixed mark
That looks on tempests and is never shaken;
It is the star to every wandering bark,
Whose worth's unknown, although his height be taken.
Love's not Time's fool, though rosy lips and cheeks
Within his bending sickle's compass come;
Love alters not with his brief hours and weeks,
But bears it out even to the edge of doom.
If this be error and upon me proved,
I never writ, nor no man ever loved.
                SONNET 116

Are We In Relationship?

Is love an "ever fixed mark that looks on tempests and is never shaken?" This is what we are promised from early childhood. The media insure that we can expect "the right one"—our soul mate—to appear, magically clothed in designer suits and cloaked in the fantasy of fulfilling our every need and desire. Yet, even the strongest tree in the forest, will shake in a boisterous wind; as do our own relationships with our companion bubble seekers.

For many the ultimate satisfaction is when we are in an intimately connected relationship with another person. Frequently we superimpose our deepest yearnings onto this being with who we are in relationship: parent, child, lover, spouse, employer, employee…we expect to be cherished at best, and truly heard at the least. Too often, we feel that our relationships are letting us down. We may grow uncomfortable when our loved ones change in ways that make them seem unfamiliar. Our friends and partners may fail to live up to our expectations, which we tend to set pretty high. The truth is, they are only uniquely themselves, undoubtedly flawed, and probably searching in similar ways. We are none of us so perfect. We can intentionally raise our vibration levels, and seek perfect divinity, but alas, most of the time we walk around in fairly ordinary realms, doing what amounts to the mundane stuff of life. Grocery shopping is neither sexy nor particularly uplifting, but it is grounding and real in the truest sense.

In order for us to see the divine perfection in ourselves and in our partner, we sometimes need to plug into the great light source of 'all that is'. Think of it as getting spiritually recharged. Remember, that because we are from the light, we must first be consciously connected to the light. Then we need to be deeply connected to our authentic, true selves. We must, in essence, be in genuine relationship with our very core being. Only then can we form genuine relationships with others. Only then can others see in us the beauty we possess. Only then we will be able to put aside our judgment and simply love openly from the heart space.

I recall a particular woman engaged in shamanic apprenticeship with me. Initially she came to learn to journey, and to receive a power animal. She had an interesting and rather eclectic spiritual background, which included an active Catholic focus, knowledge of Sufi ways, and she was also a Reiki master. Kyra is also a gifted artist and belly dancer. We spent many hours together in our sessions. She was eager to learn, articulate, communicative and truly a joy to teach. Eventually she asked for a Soul Retrieval. In this healing process, I would take the classic shamanic journey to non- ordinary reality and meet up with my power animal to find and retrieve any lost bits of her soul essence that had split off due to a previous trauma and were ready to return, and let my client be whole. Following the healing, we spent many sessions plumbing the rich fields of her newly returned and authentic self. As much as I enjoyed her as a student and client, and as much as I watched her blossom and unfold, there were two puzzling aspects to her behavior that I felt needed more attention. The first aspect related to her hesitation to use her voice for spiritual purposes. Although she had developed a good working relationship with her power animal, she was reluctant to sing.

Fear around singing can be a real impediment to a burgeoning shamanic practitioner, as singing is often an integral component to calling the spirits. Shamans employ the use of song to merge with spirit in order to move the ego out of the way– the ego that has fear, for instance. Once a clear channel, or "hollow bone" has been created, the spirits and the practitioner now merged together in this ego-less space can then perform healings and obtain helpful information. I tried many things I thought might help Kyra awaken her inner singer. Some would work a little bit, but she never seemed encouraged enough to belt out with her voice, and claim her power both as an individual and a practitioner of shamanism. Eventually my spiritual allies gave me some powerful suggestions to remedy the situation. They instructed me to have her engage in relationship building with a small plant of mine. The plant had been brought to me by another wonderful woman as a gift of love when she had her own soul retrieval. It seemed the spirits wanted this gift to grow exponentially; they had a plan. First they told me to teach her the transfiguration technique for becoming one's own divine light. After learning to transfigure into her divinity, they said she should transfigure in the presence of the plant for 7 days, with the specific intention of building relationship with it. Following that, she was to journey and ask the plant for its special song, and then she was to sing the plant's song back to it for 7 days. Ultimately, she would then journey to the plant spirit requesting she be given her own power song. We were both somewhat excited by this suggestion from non-ordinary reality, because it seemed to make a good deal of sense; however, Kyra became challenged in the execution of the spiritual exercise. She would start the process, but skip a few days in between. It took many months before she fulfilled the spirits' suggestions. There were always reasons why she had to stop the process before it was completed. Chief among them, was that she wanted privacy to do her spiritual work, and as a wife and mother she had little of either.

The other area that needed her attention was her relationship with her husband. You see, for all her good intentions around her shamanic studies, and willingness to use ritual and healing in her life, she was still unable or unwilling to tell her husband the least bit of information about her spiritual pursuits. When she came to my house for a session, she told him she was going to an art class. She had shared her Sufi and Reiki leanings with him previously, which only mystified him. He seemed shut off to that part of her. As she became more and more connected to the work of the shaman, she became more and more disconnected from him. From time to time I wondered aloud if perhaps their mutual unhappiness had something to do with the fact that he really had no idea what was going on with her. I would gently point out that as he had no idea what she was doing with her time, he wasn't really in a position to be supportive. But she reported that he was inordinately judgmental in other areas of her life as well; he questioned the subjects of her paintings, he didn't peruse the spiritual books she'd strategically leave lying around the house; furthermore, he balked when she became deeply involved with their own Catholic church, the very congregation he had chosen for the family. It seemed he rejected everything about her that spoke to her deepest core, which is to say, her very deep connection to her spirituality. Thus she was in conflict with him, and he with her; yet, he never knew the depth of the conflict because she hid her authentic self from him out of her fear! It seemed a dizzying merry-go-round from my perspective. I pondered a plan that might help.

I intuited that her reluctance to sing from her heart was connected to her reluctance to share her truest self with her husband. I felt, and the spirits agreed, that what mattered most was to be in authentic relationship with her self in order to be in authentic relationship with him. So we proceeded from that standpoint.

It is not possible to be honest with another, until we are honest with ourselves. This yearning to be authentic is frequently sabotaged—especially with women—by their reluctance to claim their power in visible and viable ways; the risk of rejection seems to override the need to be whole. I have seen this too often with my female clients. They are subjugating their authenticity to what they perceive to be their husband's preferences. My observation is that when you withhold your authenticity, you cannot expect to be supported for who it is that you are.

Connecting deeply to your core involves some risks, no question. When we change, not everyone in our lives is happy with who it is that we become. That is the way of things. Nothing is permanent. Still, to be able to say you have really given your changing relationships a fair chance at success is to be willing to connect with yourself, reveal yourself, and create a safe space for your partner to reveal himself at the moment he is ready. Remember, again, it is paramount to respect where it is we are at any given moment. And, yes, that does include acknowledging when you are in a fear space. But fear can be transmuted into something better, if you are willing to do the hard work of shifting yourself.

Being in a fear space does not give us license to circumvent who we truly are. We have these bodies and minds, these desires and dreams. It is our task, our giveback to our Creator, to ultimately give birth to *ourselves*. Denying our creativity, our songs, our words, our dances, our philosophies, or our spiritual journeys is denying the gift of life we each have received. *It is our singular responsibility to discover who we are, and then to allow that person to manifest. Moment by moment. Wherever that is.*

When I first met Kyra, she was painting female subjects who had no faces. She described this as representing all women. As art is subjective, I interpreted somewhat differently. I felt the women had no faces because she wasn't ready to reveal the full woman inside herself. Over a year passed where we were in sessions together. During that year Kyra took many journeys around the issue of her conflict ridden marriage and the power jockeying between Kyra and her husband. When she showed me her recent painting of a beautiful belly dancer, I almost cried. Her subject had a beautiful face! To me this was the evidence of real growth. At the same time, Kyra began to talk about the necessity of being more forthcoming with him. This was a powerful step. When she had been focusing on her fear, she was immobilized. When she began to focus on the living dynamic of the actual relationship, she began to embrace the possibility that she could be all she was meant to be, and improve the connection with him. *There are no guarantees, of course, but the odds on successful communication are clearly improved when both parties have the same information!*

DUKE SENIOR:
True it is that we have seen better days,
And have with holy bell been knoll'd to church,
And sat at good men's feasts, and wip'd our eyes
Of drops that sacred pity hath engend'red;
And therefore sit you down in gentleness,
And take upon command what help we have
That to your wanting may be minst'red.
                AS YOU LIKE IT Act 2, Scene 7

My Bubbles Manifest

In the preceding words of Mr. Shakespeare, he indicates that gentle help from our community can alleviate some of the worst times in our lives. This is practical, stunningly simple advice. Indeed, it is the catalyst for his presence in this book! How equitable the world which balances out our misfortunes against our successes all the time! Still, I'm sure one or two of you will agree with me that this level of fairness doesn't necessarily follow us around.

Why did I need help? Why do I care if you do? I was born a sensitive, an 'Empath'; keenly attuned to the emotional workings of those around me, viscerally affected by my immediate physical environment, and deeply susceptible to the sound of criticism and harsh words. Because I felt things so intensely, I tended to project those feelings outward, quickly earning the moniker of "Sarah Bernhardt" from my parents. Perhaps they meant it lovingly, but a childhood of hearing that you are "a little actress" tends to make you feel no one believes you, or in you; others think you're pretending, and they disregard your true experience. Having your heart ignored is hard.

The summer I was almost 5, my parents planned a European vacation for the two of them. To that end, my older brother Mark was packed off to family friends in Toledo who had three sons; my sister Louise and I were taken to my mother's sister in Brooklyn, New York. My memories of this time are distilled and frozen in portrait. To me, it felt like the family was fractured apart. I was troubled being separated from my brother, who I viewed as a kind of protector. Although I felt safe at my aunt and uncle's, I had a nagging feeling of abandonment.

The night before my parents were to leave, I accidentally managed to rip my inner arm open rather brutally on the spikes of a picket fence. The rush to the hospital, my parent's ashen faces, and the painful stitches I received remain etched in my mind to this day. The care and concern was palpable; however, in the morning, my parents left on an airplane as planned. At that point, the feeling of abandonment became crystallized; it was a very long time, indeed, before I was able to recognize the negative impact of that earlier loss.

That sense of being left behind with no protector shadowed my childhood, infused my adolescence and informed my emotional dis-ease. In shamanic as well as psychological terms, this kind of experience can be viewed as an incipient, traumatic event. The adult Frannie understands that dissociation caused from trauma can occur and become the progenitor of all manner of life difficulties. In the case of Mom and Dad flying off to Europe and leaving me, literally wounded and patched up, pieces of my childhood soul essence flew away from me. This left me unable to bear the feelings of vulnerability and loss. Of course, I didn't know anything of these matters, only that I moved through life constantly expecting to be abandoned by friends, lovers and family. We create what we speak, or imagine, and situations of abandonment materialized over and over. From childhood friendships gone sour to teenage romances that died on the vine, I seemed to be experiencing an inordinate amount of rejection and separation. I was in a lot of pain.

I sought and found solace and connection in the theatre community. That I had the ability to empathize with the pain and feelings of others was a real boon in that environment. I could will myself to feel anything any character was feeling, and I played out my personal angst on the stage. I studied and 'mastered' the art of method acting, in which you incorporate your own memories and experiences to inspire the immediacy of your character's experience. I was attracted to roles that spoke about loss and abandonment: Blanche from "A Streetcar Named Desire", Masha from "The Three Sisters", Abigail from "The Crucible".

In "West Side Story", playing Anita, I sang the heartfelt duo "I Have a Love" with the character of Maria, late in the play after we have lost both our boyfriends to death from gang violence. The fact that audience members were sniffling and blowing their noses was the most exciting thing I'd ever encountered in theatre. I'd made them cry! I was thrilled that I had made that audience connection. I'd achieved a perfect union that I experienced as a kind of bliss…I sang, I felt, I cried. They listened, they felt, they cried. At last I was communicating!

The theatre at once uplifted and imprisoned me. It allowed me to reveal myself through a variety of roles, yet encouraged me to keep repeating experiences, albeit on stage, that were painful, and hurtful.

In high school I also discovered philosophy, embracing the concepts of existentialism. I saw myself as a unique individual moving through a hostile universe and thanks to the writing of Jean Paul Sartre and my French class, I began to move beyond the realm of the emotions and started developing my mental and intellectual abilities. Suddenly I had some control. I could make choices. I was responsible for the consequences. I had free will. I was going to be authentic. I would never exhibit "la mauvaise foi"—bad faith. I would be true to myself, and true to the world.

A few adolescent explorations with psilocybin expanded my perceptions and showed me the inherent essence of everything around me. Glimpses into the spirit world while under the influence of the "magic mushrooms" taught me that there was more going on there than meets the eye. I fell absolutely in love with the natural world. Dancing fir trees, ducks that glistened, clouds that formed spinning wheels all came alive for me. The scent of the grass, the touch of the earth–these were memories of those youthful experiments that permeated my soul, and moved into my being almost on a cellular level. I became implanted with whispers from nature, but had not as yet learned how to hear those voices.

I hadn't yet moved beyond my theatrical aspirations, and spent several years in the mid 1970's as a struggling actress in Manhattan. Those were dark times in the Big Apple. We used to call it the Wormy Apple. Crime was rampant and pornography stores exploded everywhere. It was the time of the great black out and the summer of the Son of Sam. You never went out without at least a ten spot in your pocket. "Mugger money," we called it–something to give the muggers so they wouldn't become enraged and take your life out of spite.

It was also the time I entered psychotherapy, searching for some solace to my emotional upheavals and an antidote to the pervasive depression and anxiety attacks that dogged me. It was a struggle to make sense of the feelings of abandonment and rejection I still carried around with me, like a bad allergy that just wouldn't quit.

Meanwhile, my adored older brother Mark was living the hippie life in San Francisco. He took a lot of LSD, took up the guitar, climbed mountains that led to heaven and was the one person in the family that seemed okay with me just the way I was. I took several trips to visit him and his roommates, and along the way I got little life instructions from one of them, Sherrie Kimball, or Mountain Woman as I secretly thought of her. She was strong, generous, loving, and I found her fascinating. She shared a house with my brother and her lover Alex, and their little boy, Orion. From Sherrie I learned about water conservation, astrology and numerology. These last two gave me insights into myself, and validated aspects of who I was, and my delight and love for self-discovery was really initiated in those wonderful chats with Sherrie, whose friendship I still cherish.

After four years I looked around and realized I was no longer doing what I had come to Manhattan to do, i.e., perform on stage. In the interim I had become an office manager for a cemetery corporation, had taken some college classes at Columbia University, had experienced two major relationships with men, and discovered I could pay my way, support myself and build a life in New York City. The problem was, I wasn't particularly thriving in this life I'd made.

This was a heady time for the feminist movement and I was right in the thick of it. I joined a consciousness raising group, advocated the equal rights amendment and demanded equal pay for equal work. Stereotypes and long entrenched societal roles were being examined and broken down all around me.

Maybe it was the feminism and political consciousness raising. Maybe it was the fact that I wasn't acting anymore. Maybe it was the death of yet another relationship. Maybe it was a consequence of three years of therapy. It was a potent brew; I found myself, at the age of 23, six sheets to the wind drunk one evening with a group of people I had just met at a Peabody's Happy Hour after work. After politely telling the stock broker from Santa Barbara, California with whom I'd mostly been spending the evening that, in fact, I was not going to go back to his hotel room with him, I took a taxi to my apartment. There I recall I sat in my bathroom sink and had a conversation with myself in the mirror. I was pretty drunk, but I know I said, "You know, you don't have to stay here anymore." And my reflection nodded sagely, "You sure don't."

Perhaps this was an odd way to choose a major life transition; I made the choice regardless. After that I went about the business of closing my accounts, informing my landlord, selling my piano, and saying goodbye. I missed Manhattan more in those last six weeks than I ever did before or since. My path was clear. I was tired of those United States posters that showed Manhattan on the east side, California on the west side, and nothing in between but a cow or two. I didn't believe there was no life out there. In fact, I believed that my life *was* out there. My goal was simple. I would leave New York literally to discover America, and to discover myself.

After several months of interesting travels through Wisconsin, Missouri, Tennessee, and Louisiana, I landed in El Paso, Texas, where a former director, a dinner theatre, and an acting job were waiting for me. This was a memorably expansive time when great changes began to percolate inside me. The stalwart people I met in Texas, exotic trips into Mexico, instant theatre community, plus the sheer hugeness of the land mixed together to form the crucible for accelerated personal growth.

When I wasn't working as a waitress at Applegates, or performing by night at Gillespie's Dinner Theatre, I felt called to roam the wild places in the Franklin Mountains and explore the desert terrain which surrounded El Paso. I fell in love with Hueco Tanks, a seemingly desolate pre-Colombian rock habitat that revealed cave petroglyphs of a once viable shamanic life. My spirit opened to the songs of the ancients I sensed in these places. I heard the call—but did not yet know how to respond. I visited the Tigua Indian reservation and camped on the Apache Indian reservation in neighboring New Mexico, a state that is Mecca for outdoors enthusiasts. Ghost towns, cliff dwellings, abandoned shacks down horse trail roads beckoned to me and I devoured the sheer history of these places. I imagined how people lived, and woke in my sleeping bag to many a glorious sunrise in some off the beaten path location.

Even the panoramic view from my apartment balcony was of Mexico, colorful (and impoverished) villages dotting the mountainsides, with the Cristo del Rey statue perched atop one peak. There in the rugged southwest, amongst shimmering sunlight and golden hues and tough earth, I discovered a kind of aching, lonely beauty. The vast empty spaces lured me into countless hours hiking and camping in the wilderness. I even took up panning for gold in the Gila Wilderness in New Mexico, beating up my feet with blisters to reach a remote stream on a trailhead marked 666. Filling my canteen with clear, mountain spring water—standing on a dangerously narrow precipice soaring over the canyon immediately beneath me—ah, this was as exciting as standing on top of the Empire State building in my previous—now long distant—New York life.

All that quiet, empty space, those grand vistas of far off mountains, paint brush mesas, eagles gliding in patient serenity high above…These were creation's masterpieces inspiring in me a deep spiritual yearning to viscerally connect to the wellspring of life. The sights and sounds of those vast expanses began to open me in new and thrilling ways. *It's hard to resist seeing yourself in relationship to the natural world when you are so much of it.* One day, in a phone conversation with my brother in San Francisco, I said, "Hey, I'm ready for you to send me your famous spiritual growth reading list." More than glad to oblige, he mailed a list that contained great Buddhist teachings. He recommended I read Tarthang Tulku, and Chogyam Rinpoche, among others, which I did with a great hunger and respect. My perspective broadened and my awareness level began to heighten.

First, I devoured the writings of Krishnamurti's Awakening To Intelligence, which in a quirky twist of synchronicity, had been gifted to me by a lovely Iranian Muslim man with whom I'd shared a short romantic relationship. Krishnamurti's essential message was that in *order for a human being to effect outward change in her life, she needed to have an inner revolution.* I embraced that notion and my spiritual journey was officially underway.

What had I been seeking, indeed, when I chose to leave my cosmopolitan life in New York? Certainly I sought to discover my own inner landscape, but also, a connection to something deeper even if I hadn't quite known what that was then. Currently, I pursued jobs in theatre because that was what I knew, and at that point acting was the only work I still felt passionate about; yet, as the months flew by, my hunger to learn motivated me to go back to school in a formal academic way, too. Thus it was that in the dusty, west Texas town of El Paso I finally completed my B.A. in theatre at UTEP, and discovered a whole new ocean of creative vision when I began to direct plays.

In assuming the director's responsibilities, I immediately recognized that being able to visualize an entire production from concept to execution, from costumes to set design, from acting to front of house, was a far richer gold mine than anything I'd encountered as an actress. I believe to this day that directing plays fostered the skill set I needed to train my mind to visualize great endeavors in great detail. But most significantly, my connection with the concept of *manifestation* had begun. There is something very exciting and powerful about directing a play. As I've previously noted, we create what we speak. I would say: "Bleachers!" and the set crew would set about measuring planks of wood. It was directing a modest little play called "Bleacher Bums" by Joe Montegna at the El Paso Playhouse that created the opportunity for me to develop this new way of seeing.

It's a fluff of a play, about a group of disconnected Cubs fans, and the action revolves around the progress of the baseball game that they are attending. . It was mostly a character study, with very little dramatic arc. There wasn't even an intermission, just a "seventh inning stretch." The actors were largely untrained, and I was met with many a blank stare when I informed them that while their task was to create the game for the audience through their reactions to the game they were "watching", the action, per se, had to be shown through their use of subtext and continuous improvisation. My group of actors ranged in age from fifty to eleven. I had to teach them the basics of improvisation, and continued to stress throughout the rehearsal process, how important, even necessary it was for them not to only watch the game, but watch, listen and react to each other, the calls of the umpire and improvise stage business, even reacting to the weather fluctuations. Fore therein reflected the hidden undercurrents as conflicts began to creep up between the fans.

Alexander was my Assistant Director. We had met in theatre classes at UTEP and worked together successfully. Together we were a good balance, he a masculine presence, with a keen creative mind, and an ability to communicate with actors. I was the woman with the visions, who constantly motivated and challenged the company to excel. We beat a redundant drum: "You have to improvise!"

I learned an unexpected thing or two about manifestation at the company party closing night. The party was held in a trailer, which meant the rooms were close and crowded. Alex and I were somewhat befuddled most of the evening. It seemed that there was some kind of extra marital affair going on between the actress who played a character named Melanie, and the actor who was married to a real wife named Melanie. Apparently, as gossip had it, Melanie was most upset because she had just discovered this relationship between John, and the other actress. She corralled me at the kitchen sink as I did my part washing dishes, and asked me what I had seen, and what I knew, and what should she do. There had been some glances between the actress and John that I had observed, and I'd actually wondered about it a bit myself; however, I told Melanie I really didn't have any information.

Alex and I conferred about this latest development, shaking our heads and muttering, "Community theatre", delivered as an epithet of no great honor. Hours later, Alex and I were informed that we had been the recipients of a great hoax. The cast, determined once and for all to prove to us they were capable of improvisation, had deliberately staged the phony affair, starting in recent days with dressing room shenanigans and gossip. John's wife, Melanie, was in on the whole plan! We were stunned, overwhelmed, actually. They sure proved they could act off the cuff!

It was a huge compliment. They had gone to ridiculous lengths of subterfuge and deception to prove to us they had what it takes.

Looking back, it is clear that my will to manifest a company that listened to each other and responded and worked as a team was realized. I believe their goal was to have Alex and I see who they really were, when they gave free rein to their authentic creativity. It was a magnificent, and powerful event. The play was never much past average, but the party was a tour de force performance!

I had caused an inner revolution to rise up in the hearts and minds of the "Bleacher Bums" cast. To change my perception of their abilities, to prove they were more like professional actors, to stretch themselves, and to find themselves, and to be SEEN for who they truly were, they changed their own status quo. They may have come in unseasoned, amateur actors, but they left the production having ripened into stronger, better trained actors capable of focused intention and quantifiable results which would surely impact other areas of their lives.

And I was doing the same. I devoured the books my brother recommended. I relished the concept that I could choose balance in my mind regardless of circumstance. In order to effect a positive mental environment, I coud meditate on whatever emotions arose during adversity. Through this meditation, I could assert myself in my own life in new, authentic ways. I learned to break the pattern of avoidance that prevented me from recognizing my resistant as fear; that through meditation I could discern how to be effective in circumstances previously paralyzing (Tulku).

Under this Buddhist influence, I began to meditate and practice yoga daily. I even quit smoking cigarettes (the curse of theatre people).

As a result of my inner revolution, I grasped the necessity for people to feel connected together around a common goal. I learned the power of nature to heal and transform. I became someone for whom the unexamined life was not only not worth living, it had become as essential as breathing for me to examine and clarify my life's purpose so that I would evolve into my highest, authentic self.

With deep gratitude to the flora and fauna of the southwest, and to its large hearted people I returned home to Michigan after 5 years to begin the next chapter of my life. I acknowledge the gifts I received there: they came from the warmth of the people, the soaring of the eagles, the might of the mountains, the solace of the streams, the joy of the cloud formations, and the whispered secrets of the natural world…

DUKE SENIOR:
Sweet are the uses of adversity,
Which, like the toad, ugly and venomous,
Wears yet a precious jewel in his head;
And this our life, exempt from public haunt,
Finds tongues in trees, books in the running brooks,
Sermons in stones, and good in every thing.
AS YOU LIKE IT Act 2, scene 1

OBERON:
I know a bank where the wild thyme blows,
Where oxlips and the nodding violet grows,
Quite over-canopied with luscious woodbine,
With sweet musk-roses, and with eglantine.
A MIDSUMMER NIGHT'S DREAM, Act 2, scene 2

Connecting to Nature

Being disconnected is the greatest illness of our time. If we think of connections as energy currents that pass from being to being, whether human, plant, mineral or animal, then surely the greatest conductor of spiritual energy is the natural world in which we live. From the tiniest blade of grass in Manila, to the tallest Sequoia in California, there exists within each a direct relationship between each living being and its Creator. We know perfectly well we need sunlight in order to survive; but we tend to take it for granted. For many of us, our relationship with the sun goes no deeper than pondering the critical question of which SPF to buy at the drugstore. How often do you think about the sunlight it takes to grow your food? We take our water for granted, too. We open a tap and out it flows. Never mind that most of us drink chlorinated, fluoridated water with a funny taste. Never mind that most of us have no idea where to find the actual location of our local water supply. We insist on carpets of green lawn even though we waste tons of water annually when we could be planting edible foods that could feed the world, or beautiful gardens that would feed our souls instead. I wonder how many of us actually spend time having picnics or playing croquet on our lawns? I have noticed that many people complain all winter long about the cold, then turn around and crank up the thermostat on their air conditioners as soon as the temperature climbs above 72 degrees. Some people stay indoors all summer! We truly live in a state of disconnectedness from nature. *When we are disconnected from nature, we are disconnected from ourselves, because we are part of nature.*

Nature is the great healer. In nature we communicate with our essence, and connect deeply with the pulse of all that is. It's hard not to feel the energy of life buzzing around you when bees are zooming and orioles are filling the air with delightful song. I'd like to go one step further, and say that being disconnected *from nature* is the greatest illness of our time. In order to have those pristine lawns, we need to kill the grubs, and the moles that eat them. But the birds eat them too, so we have tinkered with the ecology of our yards because we think we should have perfectly flat, perfectly green expanses of lawns. Don't get me wrong, nobody loves to walk barefoot through a lush green park more than I do; it's just that people need to think a bit about where all this lushness is coming from, and what is being sacrificed to make it so.

Before switching to all organic weed and feed, I had the worst lawn on my block, no question. It's still uneven from moles and ground hog tunnels. Before the organic weed control, there were multi colored weeds that popped up everywhere. The rabbits enjoyed the buffet. Not for me, the chemical lawn. I want LIFE around me! Instead of the kind of yard I grew up with the sprinkler system, and the fertilizers, I have many beautiful perennials, all matter of saplings springing up—walnut, elm, ash, cedar, mulberry. I have beautiful butterflies that visit my gardens, and hummingbirds that sometimes drop in for a delicious buffet. Doves, and robins, cardinals and blue jays, wrens and finches, chickadees and starlings, sparrows and woodpeckers and even hawks abound. I have listened to the delightful song of the robin and I have seen opossums cleaning themselves on my back patio, and skunks rooting around for fruit. I live in a big city, on half an acre which I protect fiercely. I am on an intimate basis with every tree on my land. Even in the city, nature will take root and blossom and bring many hours of sweetness into your life, if you choose to make it so. *As with every relationship, it is not enough to regard it through your window, you need to communicate directly with it.*

When I walk out into my garden, I enter a state of connection with the primal essence of life force. There is an abundance of medicinal and culinary herbs from which I can create healing teas and wholesome foods. There are edible flowers like daisies and violets and dandelions. It is invigorating, revitalizing, and the deep connection I have with my garden is a strong motivation for me to respect the wild-life and plant life that visit each year. I have a mated pair of cardinals that fly over when I come out from the house! It thrills me that they know me.

Here is a simple exercise I learned with the Bear Tribe Medicine Society that you can utilize to increase your connection with your own yard so that you can deepen your connection to your own life force, and to "All that is", too. As my buddy Will Shakespeare wrote, "The earth has music for those who listen."

Exercise for Earth Awareness:

Find a comfortable place in nature, or in your own yard, where you will not be disturbed for a period of time. Get right down on the earth, and locate a square foot area on the ground. If able, lie on your front, allowing the heartbeat of the earth to synchronize with your heart beat. Then open all your senses, and your heart, too. Watch, listen and smell fully whatever comes into this square foot area for at least 30 minutes. You don't have to do anything. Just be, and pay attention, to whatever it is you observe. You will be amazed at how much life is going on literally under your feet every day. This is uncomplicated to do, yet can result in an evocative experience for you. Happy connecting!

Exercise to locate your power spot:

Another great way to connect deeply with the natural world is to intentionally seek out and locate a place in nature where you feel whole. You are seeking a place where you can connect with everything around you, and that includes you. This is a place in which you can begin to build a genuine relationship with nature. You are looking for a place to spend about a half hour, once a week. Again, this can be in your own yard, but it's nice if you are able to visit a wetland, park, or nature preserve. As you walk in this natural place seeking your power spot, shut off your analytical mind, and let your heart lead you to your spot. Something will draw your attention to this specific place. Perhaps you'll follow the flight of a particular bird there. Perhaps the soothing sounds of a flowing stream will beckon to you. It will be easy for you to know if THIS is the spot. Because once you arrive you will feel as if you have come home. You may even feel your body tingle and wake up.

It's good to bring a present. You can offer a little tobacco to the 6 directions (four cardinal directions, above and below), or a little cornmeal. You can bring a pretty stone or some bread for the birds. If you are empty handed, you can always leave a strand or two of your own hair. The critters and birds will find a use for it! Now that you are here, spend half an hour or so observing with all your senses. You can consciously expand your energy out to all that is around you with your intention. This is obviously a much bigger commitment than spending 30 minutes observing the same square foot area. Remember, you are a life form here as well—observe your own reactions, check into your heart. Breathe. In this exercise, the idea is to come back each week, as if you are visiting a dear friend. See how this power spot feeds you, and what you can give back. There is no right or wrong way to do this, all that matters is your intention to be in relationship with a place in nature. Nature will take care of the rest.

After you have visited your power spot for several weeks, you may feel ready for a real vision quest! Lasting anywhere from one to typically four days, your sponsor will send you out on the land to fast and commune and cry for a vision. Usually these programs are of a longer duration than the actual quest itself. People come together from all walks of life. In community, they experience the severance from their regular life before they go out by themselves for several days and nights. And there is usually an integrative aspect to the program after the quest itself has ended, in which participants have an opportunity to process and share their experiences, as they regroup their energy to reenter their regular lives. Vision quest can be the penultimate in building relationship with the natural world. On my first vision quest, I was expecting to experience my inner loneliness on a very deep level. My hope was to come to peace with how alone I felt in the world. My experience was the exact opposite; I'd never felt less alone, or more connected in my entire life! From that time forward, I have intentionally built relationship with all manner of animals, trees, plants, and, oh, yes—people, too.

Note: There are many organizations and tribal elders, too, who sponsor vision quest programs. You can refer to the End Notes for a partial list.

MACBETH:
Canst thou not minister to a mind diseas'd,
Pluck from the memory a rooted sorrow,
Raze out the written troubles of the brain,
And with some sweet oblivious antidote
Cleanse the stuff'd bosom of that perilous stuff
Which weighs upon the heart?

DOCTOR:
Therein the patient must minister to himself.
                MACBETH Act 5, scene 3

Medical Disconnection

One of the greatest disconnects in our society is the polarization of care that exists within the traditional (allopathic) medical establishment. Specialists are encouraged to focus on one aspect of an injury or illness. This tunnel vision can lead to misdiagnoses and lost cues. If your physician is a traditionalist, who seeks to treat the *injury*, as opposed to the *injured*, then it will become incumbent upon you to fill those gaps in your medical care. But how are we, mere mortals who aren't trained in the ways of medicine, to advocate for ourselves if we're not sure what we're looking for, or even what questions to ask?

We must start with a new paradigm. Holistic healing and healers treat the entire individual. We are one being, though we are made up of many connecting parts: tissues, skin, bones, vessels, organs and so forth. Like any puzzle, if you remove or damage one part, a void or disharmony remains; therefore, everything contiguous to it is affected by the disharmony. Like falling dominoes, our bodies will respond in cascading ways to our illnesses or injuries. Thus, an injury to the foot can have deep repercussions to the leg you are favoring, or the opposite leg which is now doing double duty, can experience more stress. Immobility, for example, can impact an individual's mood. The ensuing isolation can result in depression. Drugs prescribed can have unexpected or unwelcome side effects, the results of which can be debilitating and seriously escalate the whole incident. What was once an injury to one part of the body can become the primary focus of the entire human physiology depending on circumstances, and severity.

We need to pay attention to the signals our bodies are continuously sending us. We need to learn to watch for the nuances that are indicative of the contiguous domino effect, whereby one injured area affects the next and so on and so on. We need to be responsible for ourselves and proactive in our dealings with our doctors. We need to focus not only on what is happening within and without our bodies, but what is being spoken or implied in the doctor's office. It is a rather bleak indictment of our medical system that so much of our healing is by default left up to us; the reality is that if we want to have the very best of care, there is no one more on our side than ourselves. Research, stay informed, ask questions, get referrals, and by all means allow yourself to become a partner working in tandem with your doctor.

Those of us who practice shamanic healing or other healing arts are probably more accustomed to seeing the patient or client as a whole being. Because we are primarily concerned with the spiritual aspect of illness, shamanic healers tend to seek, obtain, share and heal with information that is for the person in her entirety: physical, mental, spiritual as well as emotional. Sometimes when we bring our alternative healing ideas into the allopathic or traditional doctor's office, the physician can become flummoxed by all the details, especially as they seem to veer farther and farther away from the traditional locus of the injury or illnesses. Discuss but don't confront your doctor. She is doing what she learned in medical school. In the end, it is up to us to seek and sustain those healers who will assist in strengthening our life force.

Connecting To Life Force

"All that lives must die passing through nature to eternity." W.S.

Every blade of grass has a life. From tiny seed, nourished with sacred water and sunlight, to tall green shaft, climbing ever higher towards the penultimate sun, each living being contains within its essence the driving instinct to survive. When a human comes along and lies down upon a field of grass, and takes the time to become quite still, that human can hear the grass grow. That human's heart and primal essence can connect deeply to the life force all around: in the cooling shade of trees or the drone of bees visiting the flowers. A brief respite off one's feet in a field can be much more than just a time-out. It can be an opportunity to synchronize one's heartbeat with the heartbeat of the earth itself. This life force that propels us forward is the essence of our existence. *Living in balance with the earth can only improve our time here.*

But our lives are frequently not so pastoral. Many of us spend our days utterly disconnected from the rhythm of the earth indeed many of us are disconnected from our own heartbeats. We may feel our blood racing in response to various stimuli in our environments. We may encounter the "flight or fight" syndrome in a variety of urban situations as we move throughout our days…busy with long lines, traffic jams, road rage, mountains of bills and financial obligations…yet how many of us take the time to stop. To sit. To match our pulse to the pulse of the universe…The drumming of a woodpecker…The buzzing of the cicadas…The infernal drone of our much beleaguered cousin the mosquito? Not many. Not enough.

It is the disharmony between us and the natural world around us that causes so many of us to shut down. If we are out of touch with the sound of a butterfly's wing, then we are likely to be out of touch with the sound of our partner or spouse, whining about which way the toilet paper roll faces...We have become so accustomed to background noise, that genuine silence can almost feel frightening. Clocks tick, motors whir, horns honk and trill a variety of annoying sounds, people are talking on phones glued to their ears, computers are humming, radios are blasting, brakes are screeching, and sirens are whizzing by. *We hear so many different sounds in a day, but rarely take the time to listen closely to the moments in between.* The squirrel chattering in your front yard may have something very important to say to you, and you're missing it because your television has a cute commercial about a chattering squirrel. Animals, with their instinctive drive for life, can offer us much in the way of wisdom and counsel, if we can only stop long enough to listen. Because of their intense focus on survival, they are more acutely plugged in to the subtle shifts in the elements.

Of course, there are still many of us who do stop and smell the roses, who experience twitching nostrils at a particular scent in the air, who do follow the movements of the animals, and who revere the old trees, and honor them.

"Tree huggers" is a crude epithet that is hurled like a weapon towards environmentalists and nature lovers by those who haven't a clue what it really means. These eco bullies usually have something man made that they desire which they fear will not be realized because others have placed a higher priority on the sanctity of life, whether spotted owls, turtles, salmon, or people. "Tree Hugger" has been used by those who don't have proper respect for their own ecosystem to denigrate those who do strive to create balanced ecosystems where we can all thrive. Actually, it's not a very derogatory term, it's really a beautiful term filled with love and life force.

Exercise for hugging a tree:

Go out into the woods nearest your house, even if you have to walk or drive to get there. Take a friend if you can, and do this at the same time. Take a relaxing stroll until you find a tree that seems to interest you. Don't worry about why. Allow your heart to soften and approach the tree respectfully as if you are about to meet someone important. This new relationship begins with gentleness and attention. Perhaps you can offer a strand or two of your hair which the birds that live in that tree will use in a good way for their nest. Imagine this tree is someone you love, someone who loves you. Wrap your arms around this beloved being, close your eyes, and relax into the embrace. Stay like this awhile and give yourself permission to just be. Even if you don't notice anything, even if you can only feel the bark scratching against your face, even if your legs grow weary and you think this whole thing is a ridiculous charade, urge yourself to stay with it for at least fifteen minutes. You may notice different sensations. You may feel your breathing and pulse slow down; this is normal, because your life force is realigning to the rhythm of the tree. You may also notice vibrant sensation; your body may be waking up as you hold yourself closely to this being. This is normal, too, because you are responding to the strength of the life force of the tree. Stay with the tree as long as you like. You may close your eyes and ask the tree to reveal its spirit to you. Accept whatever comes, whether it is an inner knowing, a picture in your mind, or a voice that comes into your head or heart.

After you and your partner have each individually done this exercise for a quarter hour or so, you may wish to extend it further. Walk away from your tree several feet. Your partner will tie on a bandanna as a blindfold for you, and turn you around a few times until you haven't any idea in which direction you are facing. Next, see if you can still identify the location of your tree! You can call out, "Where are you?" Then you must quiet your mind and breath and listen with your inner knowing for the answer. Then, with your partner to guide you safely, see if you can walk to your tree. If you have found your tree, be sure to extend a "thank you" to the life force of the tree. Then you can assist your partner in the same way.

You may want to experiment with this exercise on different occasions. If you don't "get" the tree's spirit, or if you can't locate your exact tree while blindfolded this doesn't mean you have failed, or that you aren't connected, or that you aren't any "good" at this. Remember, as in any relationship, your intention is the key. Besides, it takes time to get to know each other and build trust. It might be beneficial to try this exercise again with the same tree. Perhaps over time the tree will feel your pure intent and reveal itself to you. But even if you never experience a mutual connection, the fact that you are open to the possibility will awaken other nature spirits to your presence. Once you open to one of them, the others will recognize you as an ally. *It is always good to have friends.*

Some pigeons, Davy, a couple of short-legged hens, a joint of mutton, and any pretty little tiny kickshaws, tell William cook.
                    HENRY IV, PART 2: Act 5, scene 1

Unquiet meals make ill digestions.
                    COMEDY OF ERRORS, Act 5, scene 1

I am a great eater of beef, and I believe that does harm to my wit.

Food Culture and Life Force

Once upon a time, Nature and humans lived in harmony. Humans used to be able to communicate at will with the trees, flowers, herbs, and animals. The tribal shaman would send her spirit out to meet the spirits of these beings to obtain information about healing ways, weather patterns, and the location of the herds for hunts. Over the generations since we have been "civilized", our species has forgotten how to communicate with the natural world. Our increasingly mechanized societies have separated us more and more. Once, farmers planted each tiny seed by hand, with nothing more than a stick to poke a hole and a dead fish for fertilizer. Now seeds are planted by machines driven by people who sit atop them, far removed from the soil. In the same way, we used to harvest each ear of corn by hand, touching them to find the freshest, ripest, most nutritious food for our families. Now, when not done by machines, our food is often harvested by strangers; migrant workers whose thoughts are probably not, "This is a beautiful ear of corn, I will feed it to my child and she will grow big and strong". The worker's thoughts are probably more like, "Can I even make a living wage picking this food for this ridiculously small amount of money?"

Too many people handle your food from the time it is harvested until the time it reaches your table. And each person who handles your food, from the picker to the packer to the hauler to the stock person, is bringing their own individual energy to bear. The picker with the cold, the packer with the nagging bill collector, the hauler with road rage, and the stock person who may be having a psychological melt down may be leaving imprints of their own negativities and frustrations on your food. *Your mom was right about washing your food first!* It is best not to eat the grapes—even the organic ones—until you've given them a good wash at home.

Our whole food culture reflects the many ways we are disconnected from our food source. Meat is something that arrives neatly packaged in non-bio-degradable Styrofoam containers under plastic wrap and has frequently been died to look redder and 'fresher'. Many people can go for decades if not a whole lifetime without even seeing a cow; but this is not how it always was. In a traditional hunt, the shaman would use his spiritual skills to locate the deer, elk, or buffalo herd. Together the community would ask the spirits for assistance, and thank the animals for the life force they were abdicating so that the people could live. The animals would be butchered with the intention of utilizing every bit of it, so that the animal's spirit would live on in every conceivable way. Nothing would be wasted. Hides were tanned and turned into clothing, packaging, and shelter. Bones were used for sewing, tools, even weapons for the next hunt. Internal organs were eaten or parts of them used for water bags. Horns became instruments, or serving bowls. When you live a life that is completely connected to your natural environment you find myriad ways to best use the gifts that the universe provides for you.

Yet one must eat! So it's off to the grocery store we go, and happy to do so. Our modern life affords us every convenience. Still, it is important that we have some awareness of our food supply. We can climb into our gas guzzling SUVs, drive to the local shopping center, load up our food cart with packaged meats and canned vegetables, boxes of sugary cereals and dyed apples; but we can do so with some wisdom of the older way. We can stop a moment and think about what life was like when we had to grow our own food and learn to identify which berries were healthy, and which were toxic. We can wonder, for a moment, how it is that some mushrooms will nourish us, while others will poison us. We can reflect, at the next traffic jam, on how it is that the health food stores know just which herbs to stock, and which have cautionary labels affixed.

Just this act of reflection is an act of opening our hearts and minds to building a better connection with the natural world, and subsequently with our own life force.

Many of us work with the earth, growing things, whether food, flowers, plants or trees. People who do this kind of work describe it as "fun, healing, therapeutic". A super quick way of connecting with the life force of your own yard is to plant something in it. The act of turning the earth and getting on your knees in close proximity is surprisingly rewarding. Dirt gets under your nails, and your arthritic joints may be creaking, but when you put the final pat on the soil around the plant, there is a satisfaction that is rich like nothing else. Even if you are an urban apartment dweller, you can take a few pots and grow your own culinary or medicinal herbs in a sunny window, patio or balcony. When you harvest these herbs there is a tremendous feeling of fulfillment. When you crumble the herb into a hot cup of water for tea, you are connecting to the life force in a visceral way. Very powerful!

What is all this about the life force anyway? Don't you know you're alive? Don't you arise each morning, grab a cup of coffee and head off to work as a fully living breathing individual? Yet, even as their lungs move in and out many people don't fully utilize their respiratory system. A fully oxygenated body is a stronger, healthier and calmer system. Those eastern mystics and yogis knew a thing or two about *prana* (breath).

Exercise to breathe fully:

If you have a few minutes right now, put down this book and sit quietly. Exhale fully, so that your diaphragm begins to collapse. Then inhale slowly and deeply, filling your diaphragm first and then feel your lungs begin to swell with beautiful life giving air. Now exhale again, slowly, from the diaphragm first. Become aware of the passage of air in and out of your nostrils. Practice this for several moments. Feel your mind calm and your body quiet. Wonderful! This is how the actors and opera singers and even athletes breathe: fully, deeply.

Air is the breath of life. It is the wind that lifts us onto the wings of energy. When I am outside, I like to drink in the smells I sense in the air.

The wind carries many aromas to us from the natural world. When you smell the perfume of flowers in the air, it is the flower that is greeting you, making contact, saying hello (Andrews). I especially love the pungent smell of wet earth after a light rain shower, as if our earth Mom is so happy to have been kissed by the life giving water from above, she releases her delicious fragrance. I recall one summer afternoon when the most tantalizing, sweet scent was suddenly carried on a light breeze and rested on my nostrils. I was in my back yard, and began to follow the direction of the smell, curious to discover who was greeting me. The previous summer, a large fir tree had been struck by lightning and fallen over. There, in the clearing newly made by the fallen tree, was the sweetest wisteria vine climbing over a mulberry hitherto blocked by the towering fir. Such a luscious smell! And such beautiful blossoms. Heavenly.

I think it is good, moreover, necessary to stop and give acknowledgment to the messages carried to us in the air. From noticing the acrid smell that precedes a thunderstorm, to the delicate fragrance of a neighbor's lilac bush…like everything else, it is important for us to pay attention. Stop, listen, look, inhale. The more connected we are to the messages our senses can bring to us, the more aware we will be of what is transpiring in our environment. My brother, Mark Goldstein, used to say to me, "It is carelessness karma to ignore early warnings." *Nature always sends a sign when something big is about to occur.* Volcanoes rumble, wind begins to whip up, animals begin to take flight. When Indonesia, Thailand, and other countries in Asia experienced the 9.5 Richter scale earth quake in December of 2004, the local people said that the animals all fled for higher ground, and most survived the devastating Tsunami that killed nearly 300,000 people. There was a synchronicity between the exodus of the animals and the gathering force of the Tsunami.

ANTONY:
Sometime we see a cloud that's dragonish;
A vapour sometime like a bear or lion,
A towered citadel, a pendant rock,
A forked mountain, or blue promontory
With trees upon't that nod unto the world,
And mock our eyes with air. Thou hast seen these signs;
They are black Vesper's pageants.
              ANTONY AND CLEOPATRA, Act 4, scene 14

HAMLET:
Nothing either good or bad but thinking makes it so.

Synchronicity and Prayer by Decree

It's funny how sometimes things just work out. Plans fall into place, and surprising coincidences occur. For example, today I had a major project in the garage which entailed moving boxes and furniture and discovering many items in the process. Earlier this morning, while working on the Bibliography for this book, I realized I had no citation for Jean Sartre, most of my books having been destroyed in the Fire of 1995. As I worked in the garage, I swept and made piles of things to keep, throw or file. I came across a loose leaf filled with my childhood poems and stories. At the very top of the pile, nicely toasted, was a paper I had written years ago, complete with Bibliography. The paper, *en Francais,* was called "La Mauvaise Foi" (Bad Faith). The wisdom gained in Paula Brown's French classes at Southfield High School has only expanded exponentially over time. The exact citation I needed was right in front of me. We call this kind of coincidence *synchronicity.*

Merriam-Webster's Collegiate Dictionary, 10th Ed, defines synchronicity as "the coincidental occurrence of events and especially psychic events...that seem related but are not explained by conventional mechanisms of causality". Indeed, the very essence of synchronicity suggests a deeper meaning is involved.

The idea is that once a particular energy is activated in your life you will begin to observe moments of synchronicity related to that energy, especially if you seek and pay attention. It's rather like the old saw about pregnant women, that is when a woman is pregnant it seems she sees pregnant women everywhere. Part visualization, part prayer, aspects of synchronicity will occur when you open to them. These are little gifts from the universe that show you the wondrous ways in which all things are woven together. An obvious place to look for examples of synchronicity moving in your life is out in nature. One of my favorite memories occurred on a road trip my then 16 year old son and I took to the Upper Peninsula in Michigan. He was driving, and I was musing aloud about a shamanic journey I had taken that morning. I journeyed sometimes with the drum, and sometimes with the rattle. That morning had been a rattle journey, and I said to him, "I think I've concluded that rattle journeys are deeper journeys than those with the drum." At that precise moment I glanced out the window and saw a magnificent eagle sitting at the very top of the passing pine tree. Eagle is one of my power animals, and I said, "Guess the eagle agrees with me!" We spent a week on this trip, camping, hiking and living out of doors. Many of the places we visited were really off the beaten path. Although we saw a lot of wildlife, that was the only eagle sighting of the entire trip!

On the more mundane level, when I was producing and directing stage plays at Pinckney High School, I made a habit of visualizing and praying for items we needed for the set or costumes or props. I would verbalize what I needed beginning with, "Thank you for…." When I produced "Play It Again, Sam" by Woody Allen I needed an entire kitchen. So I began to decree, "Thank you for providing us with a kitchen for the show". Within a day or two, one of my students informed me that one of the English teachers had kitchen cabinets and counters in her basement, having recently renovated her kitchen. A day later a refrigerator appeared. Similarly, when the play was the Victorian Ibsen drama "Hedda Gabler," I discovered several antique Victorian calling cards at a local flea market which I gave to the actors. They were small props that the audience wouldn't even notice, but the actors carried them and it helped them go deeper into their characters.

When the facets from the different corners of your world begin to align, this is synchronicity helping you forward.

I believe that we must ask for the things that we need in life, from people and from our source of light, or Creator-God. "Ask and ye shall receive" is the saying, and it is true. Sun Bear, the visionary who brought back large scale medicine wheel gatherings to North America, used to teach that the best way to pray was by saying, "Thank you" for what you needed, *as if you had already received it.* Noted spiritual teacher

Sandra Ingerman also teaches the importance of the power of manifestation, as opposed to request. And of course, wasn't it Jim Morrison of the Doors who sang with such passion, "You cannot petition the Lord with prayer"? (It was, indeed.)

Think about it. When we are saying, "Please send me a kitchen", we place ourselves in the role of supplicant. We are begging. We seem weak. There isn't much strength behind that energetically. Conversely, "Thank you for the kitchen" makes it a done deal. There is a power in the presence of those words. We create what we speak. We all grew up playing at magic at one time or another, waving the proverbial wand and saying, "Abracadabra"; the origin traces the word's etymology to the ancient Hebrew (Winkler 67). The phrase so popular with children and magicians alike, Ab'ra K'dab'ra, literally translates as "I create what I speak." Thus, prayer by decree, as opposed to petition, plus visualization sparked by our imagination, combine together to foster the essence of manifesting our dreams. This manifestation may reveal itself to us through the many aspects of synchronicity moving in our lives if we but—again—pay attention to what is happening.

The more attention we give to something, the more energy is activated around it. Synchronicity is the movement of the energy of manifestation.

HAMLET:
What a piece of work is a man, how noble in reason, how infinite in faculties; in form and moving how express and admirable, in action how like an angel, in apprehension how like a god: the beauty of the world, the paragon of animals! And yet to me what is this quintessence of dust? Man delights not me--nor woman neither, though by your smiling you seem to say so.
                    HAMLET, Act 2, Scene 2

The Human Condition

Part of the human condition is the need to seek other humans with whom we can connect, with whom we can *delight*. In the animal kingdom, many species bond and mate for life; we are one of them. We possess something I consider to be an empathic response. When we encounter others whose experiences mirror our own, we are drawn to those people. Like seeking like, as it were; thus, the family of origin provides a kind of safety net for many people. Holiday gatherings, weddings, funerals, graduations and the like provide opportunities for the family unit to come together to reconnect. Our families inspire memories of more carefree days, affection and sentiment. Or they inspire the hope of deepening our relationships with far-off relatives. This can often be a revitalizing time for many fortunate people. Such gatherings often provide a barometer against which we can assess our personal growth as we report on our lives. For some solace is experienced, balm against the storm of everything else; but, just as often it is a traumatic time.

Dysfunction runs rampant through the modern American family these days, of that there is no doubt. Just ask any of your co-workers or friends, one or ten or so are undoubtedly going to acknowledge belonging to the dysfunctional family club. In fact, so many people today are estranged from their family of origin that some never see their families at all. Sometimes, the price for authenticity seems too much to pay. Others have learned to keep the peace by suppressing their truest selves when around those who love and judge them most dearly.

So where do we go to connect with those who will not judge us, who will honor our true selves? Many kinds of families exist…community groups can often forge bonds that seem more important to us. Spiritual groups can provide a refuge, or support system often lacking with our own brothers and sisters. What seems clear to me is that we all need to have people with whom we can connect, relax, and be ourselves, with whom we can share our visions, hopes, fears and losses. *Humans were not meant to be living in an alienated state.* Isolation breeds depression, which runs counter to everything we are trying to achieve in order to live a fully actualized, joyful and authentic life.

In the healing work I do with soul retrieval, I often suggest that clients bring someone along to the healing session. This person can act as a witness adding more power to the experience; also, the witness serves as a support person who can accompany the client afterward, providing a sounding board, companion, or whatever is really needed. Despite this, I continue to hear the same response: "There really isn't anyone I can bring to something like this". This saddens me, because it speaks to the great disconnect there is between who we are, how we want to be, and the expectations projected onto us by so many of the people who populate our individual lives. I believe it is hugely important that we find people with whom we can be ourselves to share and discuss and *delight in* what matters most to us. This is not always easy, I grant that. I have firsthand knowledge about just how challenging it can be. But I think it is worth persevering in our search for like-minded company. I have had many conversations with my own mother about this very matter. I had been saying that the people in my shamanic support system tend to be long distance. Many of the people whose counsel I most treasured were far away geographically. My mother always countered by suggesting I join a local synagogue which seemed counterintuitive at that time. (Mom wasn't far off the mark as it turned out later, when the merging of my Judaic and shamanic callings became as essential to me as breathing; but, the story of that merge will be told another time). In any case, the idea is to find someone, somewhere, with whom we can share a meal, a conversation, or if you're like my clients, a healing session.

At the same time, I'd like to remind the reader that we are never truly alone. To find answers we only need to walk out of doors. The wind, the rain, the sun, the birds, the animals we encounter all have something to mirror back to us, if we take the time to slow down and genuinely connect with these beings. Many years ago, when I went out for my first vision quest with the Bear Tribe, near Spokane, Washington, I had been asked to fill out a questionnaire that endeavored to discover my motivations for seeking to be out on the land alone for four days. Two parts of that questionnaire still resonate in my memory. One, asked what was my greatest fear about going out alone? I remember I wrote back that I feared that my having had this experience was going to further alienate me from other people I knew (like family members) who already deemed my spiritual pursuits to be "different" enough. The other asked what I hoped to gain. I wrote that I hoped to be able to come to some terms with how lonely I was and to be able to finally accept my singularity in this world.

Once by myself on Vision Mountain, I realized that I wasn't alone at all. There were chipmunks that scurried in and out of my sacred quest circle, and eagles circling lazily above me. I also heard the croaking ravens, and the sounds of the distant drum from the quest support group that echoed my own heartbeat back to me. I saw that the clouds were communicating directly with me, that the wind was whispering my own name. In short, I never felt less alone, or more connected than I did at that time. *Nature, they say, is the great healer, and this is undoubtedly so.*

HORATIO:
O day and night, but this is wondrous strange!

HAMLET:
And therefore as a stranger give it welcome.
There are more things in heaven and earth, Horatio,
Than are dreamt of in your philosophy.
                HAMLET Act 1, scene 5

Power Animals

In traditional shamanic societies, it was thought that everyone had a power animal from birth, welcomed and expected; otherwise, there would be no protection, and people would suffer misfortune. In those societies, humans and animals were closely connected…humans would read animal signs to locate hunting grounds, water, and other survival tools. For example, we learned which plants could heal us from observing Bear, a great healer in the animal world. We learned how to read weather and natural disaster signs by noting the behavior of the animals. Just prior to the unexpectedly destructive earthquake and subsequent tsunami in 2004, elephants and other animals were seen moving systematically to higher ground. Despite all of the devastation to humans, no major signs of animal loss were reported. *Animals know what we do not and they will show us if we pay attention.*

It is good to be in relationship with one or more helpful power animals. The power is in their willingness to protect and advise you. The stronger your relationship is, the more personal the protection. When your intentions are communicated clearly, the greater the help your power animal will be to you. Not all Power animals stay with you forever. Sometimes they come to help with a very specific issue, and are no longer needed after a time. Sometimes they feel ignored by you and eventually wander off. Having, knowing and being in relationship with your power animal will ensure its continued presence and assistance in your life. This is the bedrock of shamanic practice. I have observed that clients are fascinated with the idea of having a power animal, or protective spirit guide. Not everyone is willing to allow them-selves to pursue a working relationship. For some it smacks of "paganism". Others just can't suspend disbelief. *But the power is in your relationship, your level of connection to your spirit helper.*

A reputable shamanic practitioner can arrange to retrieve your power animal for you, and teach you how to build and sustain relationship so that you will receive the benefits from this special, ancient connection between humans and animals. We can teach you the importance of dancing your animal and how to find and use your power song for healing yourself. You can learn how to perform the classic shamanic journey, in which you travel directly to your power animal's home in non-ordinary reality to obtain information to assist in the betterment your own life, visions and dreams.

You can work with your power animal on your own behalf, or you can take these teachings to another level, and learn to work with your animal on behalf of other people, the environment, or community. Shamanic studies all require your ability to journey and have a strong relationship with your power animal as a prerequisite for advanced teachings. The most powerful aspect of being in relationship with my animal helpers is the certain knowledge that I am not alone as I make my way through the minefield of life. So, yes, I am in relationship.

It is good to merge with one's power animal routinely so the animal will want to stay with you. Through song and dance, accompanied by rattle or drum, you can call your animal to you, and merge together. While you are experiencing the non-ordinary reality connection by traveling to your animal's home, for example, your animal is enjoying the sensation of the human experience here in ordinary reality (Harner 68).

For some shamanic practitioners, there may be many power animals, a mini menagerie, and the task of dancing all these animals on a routine basis can seem intimidating. With the greatest respect to the great healers and teachers of shamanism, I'd like to suggest that sometimes it's better to forego "the rules", and let the intention of your own heart and soul be a personal guide to you in the best ways to establish a connection and maintain a successful relationship with your power animal. For these purposes, a successful relationship is one where you trust your own ability to interpret your journeys, you trust that the information revealed to you by your power animal is true, and you work comfortably as a team for divination or healing purposes whether for yourself or on behalf of others. I always tell my students and clients that building and maintaining a relationship with your power animals and upper world teachers is very much like establishing a relationship with a fellow human traveler.

One of my important spiritual teachers is a beautiful, blue-sparkly woman in human form whose name is Beta Star. She is a microcosm of many of the great female healers and teachers, and had informed me that at various times she had incarnated as Mary, mother of Jesus, as well as the Egyptian goddess Isis, among others. Her home is a magical meadow, filled with asters in shades of purple. A bench made of white stone is a place we often sit and chat. In one particular journey, I was so eager to make contact with her, that as soon as I saw her I excitedly began asking my questions. She became quite stern with me, which surprised me, and she told me, "Stop. Wait. Hello? It's nice to see you. Don't be in such a rush you forget basic manners!" Chastized, I quickly apologized and gave her a proper greeting, which she gladly shared back with me, and then the journey continued. This was a key lesson for me, and from that time forward, I am always careful to say, "Hello", before making requests from my spiritual teachers and animals. Likewise, it's proper to say, "Thank you and good-bye" when the journey ends. Good manners begin in kindergarten and never go away!

Once, sitting with a familiar group at our Midwest Peacemaker's retreat, I was sharing one of my journeys as part of the circle, regarding a particular focus the group had taken that day. As I spoke, I enumerated the information gleaned from one of my power animals who I mentioned by name. I clearly remember the astonishment of several people in my circle—a circle filled with experienced, focused and dedicated shamanic practitioners—"Your power animals have names?" I was asked. "Why, yes," I replied. "How did you get to know their names?" My simple answer, "I asked them."

I cannot over emphasize the simple power there is in a name. As an ad hoc numerologist, I do have a healthy respect for the energy embedded in names; perhaps this is why it came so easily to me. In any case, when I start working with new animals and spirit teachers, I find it most helpful to introduce myself and to ask for a name. It narrows the gap between us, and we enter into a more personal level of communication. Interestingly, I've noticed that power animals often have very mundane names, like Howard, or Ralph...and upper world teachers (who tend, at least for me, to be heroic figures or gods/goddesses) have the more exotic names. For others, it is simply Elephant, or Gazelle.

Aside from preliminary introductions and common sense etiquette, there are several simple things I do to maintain relationship with my spiritual assistants. Each morning I greet the day with a simple ritual. I go outside, regardless of the weather, fill the bird feeders, and make a tobacco offering to the spirits of the four directions, the Elementals, Earth Mother, Creator, and to all my power animals and spirit teachers. I give thanks for the gift of my life, for safety and prosperity, for right action, relationship and livelihood, and for mental, emotional, spiritual and physical healing and well-being for myself, my family of origin, my spiritual family, my students and clients past and present, co-workers, friends, and any one who has asked me to pray for them. I include a prayer for all suffering and sentient beings to come into their highest health and happiness and a prayer for peace on earth. I may include a prayer for the positive outcome of something special. I set my intention to go safely and smoothly through this day. Finally I merge with my true self, and my power animal.

The sun may not yet be up, but I have greeted and acknowledged all of my spiritual assistants. I am comforted knowing they have been reminded of me, and will be with me.

I'm an avid walker and hiker, and I've discovered that the rhythmic movement can shift me into trance; on these occasions, I may put out a call to "Whichever power animal would like to merge with me right now". I remain open as a hollow bone, and it is through observation of how my gait shifts, where the center of my gravity goes, and changes in my visual and auditory perception that I become aware of which animal has merged with me at that moment. Believe me, there is a vast difference between the gait of an elephant and that of a deer! This is another way I can create opportunity for my power animals to visit me and the world of ordinary reality. It is an enjoyable experience for both of us.

Of course, there are simple things we can do to indicate our attention is being given to our power animals. We can wear jewelry and clothing with their picture, we can place and honor their totems on our altars. Merely looking at your altar can activate these energies, just as lighting a candle or incense awakens the power. I try to look at my altars, photos and objects that represent my spiritual assistants often as I move through my day.

Thinking about your power animal, and spending attention this way is also powerful, as well as singing their power songs. Frequently when I'm walking I'll find myself humming one or another animal's songs, which can bring them right to me. I've also found that plain old conversation can be very valuable.

Once, on vision quest in the rainforest of Alaska, I became quite lost. Brant Secunda, the renowned Huichol Shaman, and founder of the Dance of the Deer Foundation, had put us out to quest with the instruction to be back at dawn, and admonished us particularly not to be late. Brant was quite firm in his notions of timeliness, and I didn't want to be the one who held up any step in the return process. I was certainly awake at dawn. Under heavy cloud cover I had started out in what I thought was towards the east, and the road. Unfortunately, my effort wasn't correct! It was still early, and there was no sound of a distant car to give me direction. A grey mist hung over the rain forest. After some determined wandering, and perhaps 45 minutes, it dawned on me that I was completely lost. I found myself literally in the middle of a blueberry thicket which is a great place to find Bear. I had already seen an actual bear on this adventure from the safety of my vision quest circle. Now I was trying to stay balanced on a very large fallen tree trunk, after having already sunk a foot into the thick underbrush beneath it. Just before, I had lost my balance and grabbed for the closest object at hand. That turned out to be a plant someone later told me was called Devil's Claw. By now, with my hand stinging from dozens of thorns courtesy of the plant, my feet aching in borrowed hiking boots (don't ask), and absolutely no idea which way was "out", I began to feel anxiety rise perilously inside me. I made my way slowly across the tree trunk to a flat area beneath a grove of pines. Here I wondered miserably why I couldn't have found this lovely place for my vision quest rather than the Kamikaze mosquito palace I'd selected earlier. I sat down on another fallen log, feeling rather desperate now. I worried about being late back to camp, and reasonably sure that if I had to wait for the sound of a passing automobile, itt could be hours, or perhaps days...that's when I started crying out, "Kauyumari!" This is Huichol for Deer. "Kauyumari! I'm lost, and I'm hurting and I need to find the road!" I kept at this for several minutes, and then, like a miracle, suddenly a strong shaft of sunlight shot down through the trees. I burst into tears of gratitude. Never have I been more appreciative of nature's compass, for this sunlight surely meant east, and east surely meant the road. The really funny part, was that as I moved off in the direction of the sunbeam, which ultimately did lead me to the road, I realized I'd never really been very far from it. But the dense thicket and jungle growth of the rainforest had completely hidden it from view; it was Kauyumari, who had been with me through much of my vision quest, who showed me how to get out, *because I asked*. Similarly, our life direction can often be obfuscated, but our power animals can steer us out of the miasma of self-doubt towards clarity. As I mentioned previously, where there is synchronicity, there one can find the divine.

As it turned out I was still late, but so were two or three others. As I trudged the mountain road back to our circle, barefoot and blistered by now because wearing borrowed hiking boots is probably the single most stupid thing I've ever done, I finally heard the welcome engine of a car. It was driven by one of the assistants from our group: Brant had sent her to round up those of us who were late or lost. Assuring them I'd been lost, not lazy, I finally made it back and received my welcome hand shake from Brant. I am sure, though, that had I not called on Kauyumari's intervention at that pivotal moment, I would have been wandering like Moses in the desert for a very long time!

HAMLET:
There is special providence in the fall of a sparrow. If it be now, 'tis not to come; if it be not to come, it will be now; if it be not now, yet it will come. The readiness is all.
                    HAMLET, Act 5, scene 2

Rituals

Writing this manuscript has alternately flowed effortlessly, or been blocked up persistently depending on my state of readiness. It is astonishing how slowly the creative process can unfold at times. It's almost too easy to set aside one's writing to attend to other matters, some truly imperative, others merely a diversion from the necessary task at hand. I confess, were it not for the intervention of my helping spirits and many outdoor breaks, I would have become lost in my direction, and probably mired in the quicksand of my own inertia. I often ponder how other authors manage to complete what they finish. With every page, I have wondered truly, where am I going with these words? Who will read them? Why am I doing this?

The answers to these and other annoying questions that plague and interrupt me do not always become clear. In the end, all that matters is that I trust in my vision, and trust in my helping spirits to guide my way. All else falls to the wayside. Thus when there is nothing inspirational left in my well, I turn back to journeying. I was told that this chapter on rituals was to be included: "Write about rituals, how important it is for people to connect to them, the power of them, and how they come about as a consequence of awareness and attention."

Although we don't always notice, many rituals that range from the sublime to the mundane surround our lives. For some, the day does not begin without the "ritual" cup of coffee. For others, the day does not begin or end without a prayer. In between, there is a vast opportunity for us to connect with a familiar pattern. There are rituals that surround the passages of human life such as Baptisms, Bar Mitzvahs, Communion, Confirmation, graduation, weddings, retirement, and funerals; these are just the most obvious.

For our purpose here, let us explore those self-generated or spirit led rituals which augment the mundane, and enhance our experience of connecting our own essence to something greater than ourselves. We shall do this by examining several specific components of ritual:

- *Rituals are important because they make us feel connected to the ebb and flow of life.*

They frequently involve other beings, who bear witness to key moments. This lends credence and depth to our actions. Additionally, through enactment of healing ritual, in particular through repetitive enactment, we are capable of realigning our thoughts from a negative state to a positive outcome. How many of you are smokers, or reformed smokers? I am in the ranks of those who used to smoke religiously, and I choose that word carefully. There was a kind of ritual to the whole gestalt around smoking. The cigarette case, the lighter, the woman's hand placed just so on the gentleman's hand who was lighting her cigarette, the lighting up after a delicious dinner, and so on. Interestingly, in the process of quitting (April 6, 1982!), I discovered a whole new set of rituals. Making a check mark on a slip of paper tucked into my cigarette case after each one I smoked encouraged me to let more time go by between each cigarette. Brushing my teeth after meals helped to calm the craving, and reminded me that the next cigarette would foul that fresh breath feeling…and for me, what turned into the most healing ritual of all… my daily Hatha yoga sessions which calmed my mind and replaced my addiction for cigarettes with my reliance on gentle *asanas* and breathing techniques. Through repetition of these new rituals surrounding my goal of Not Smoking, I was able to release my desire to smoke altogether, thus replacing the negative with the positive.

- *Rituals are powerful because they embrace our ability to transform ourselves and our environment.*

Many of our self-defeating characteristics stem from nothing more substantial than habit. Habits are learned things, and they can be unlearned often with the assistance of a well-constructed ritual. Once a negative characteristic has been quantified—whether through the shamanic journey, as is my method—or through guided meditation or another construct—a ritual specifically designed to replace the negative with something healing can provide opportunity for one to give focused awareness and attention to the issue. Through repetition and concentrated focus, we can literally reorient our minds to think in new and unexpected directions. These rituals can be self-generated, or they can be given to us directly from the spirits. I think the latter carry an inherent power because we know they are coming to us directly from those beings that most have our best interests at the fore.

Exercise To Transform a Negative Pattern Through Ritual:

This exercise is designed in two steps to help you get in touch with a negative habit or thought pattern that you would like to see changed for the better. **Step one:** Your intention is to learn what is the *most* detrimental negative habit or thought pattern that is preventing you from moving forward at this time in positive and life affirming ways. You may be shown several…Be sure to seek the one that is at the core of all the others. You can journey this intention.

For those who are meditating or visualizing, you can put on some beautiful music that helps you to relax. Breathe deeply and slowly and allow your body to release any tension it may be feeling. Take as long with this as you need until you feel centered and peaceful. Ask for the light of the Creator, or for the Light of Love to illuminate your heart and spirit. Ask for this light to spotlight for you a negative habit or thought pattern that has prevented you from being in your joy…be careful not to discount or censor what is revealed…seek the one that is at the core of all the others. Repeat step one until you have seen the truth that should resonate quite strongly for you before continuing on to the next step.

Step two is either to journey or meditate on how to construct a simple ritual that can assist you in moving from this negative habit or thought pattern to a positive place through the power of transformation. You can do this on your own, but sometimes it is interesting to have someone else learn this ritual and then to share with you how to enact it. I first experienced the power of this technique with Sandra Ingerman in her workshop on shamanic soul retrieval. Sandra suggested that we ask for a "prescription for a ritual", and to include how often the ritual is to be performed. Because there is no "time" as we know it in non-ordinary reality, you may be shown the duration through seasons, or number of moons, etc. I recall the rituals that we received for each other were varied, and exciting. Some were fun and playful, others serious and intense. All were exactly what the individual most needed to do to make the shift from negative outlook to optimistic state of being. One woman was instructed to bathe with a rubber ducky and other bath toys, and to delight in simple childish pleasure to help move her from a chronic state of being overly serious. One man was instructed to carry rocks in his pockets for a year to help him become more grounded.

The ritual I received for my partner was that she was to twirl a daisy between her fingers every day for a period of so many weeks; she especially liked it as daisies were her favorite flower…the one she received for me was also simple but most effective. I had identified my core negative habit at that time as experiencing a lack of trust in myself. Her prescription for me was to place a smudge bowl of burning sage on the floor. Then, holding my arms crosswise across my chest (i.e. hugging myself), I was to dance three times around the bowl, while humming or singing and focusing on the words "I trust myself, I trust myself." I was told to do this at least four days a week for a period of a few months.

I discovered it took very little time of my day to enact this ritual, and I liked how it made me feel so much that I did it almost every day, instead of just four days in the week. At the end of the prescribed time, I was almost sorry to let it go. There is no doubt whatsoever that the repetition of this ritual had a tremendous influence on my ability to move into a place of self-trust. While the sage was wafting away the negative thought patterns, the side to side dance step I used was imprinting my body with the new paradigm represented by my little song, "I trust myself, I trust myself". The sound of my voice gave weight and meaning to the words. The attention I gave to creatively changing my own mental state resulted in a more joyful and trusting self. Certainly this book would not have been able to exist otherwise.

- *Rituals evolve out of awareness and attention to the energies within and outside of our-selves. "As Within, So Without".*

Once you have discovered how helpful these simple rituals can be in shifting your energy from the negative to the positive, you can work with this construct as often as necessary. When a new and larger sweat lodge was built on my land new people came and new energies mixed with our established community. I quickly discovered that having my home filled with many new people eating, talking, and emotionally processing after our ceremony left a lot of chaotic energy ricocheting off the walls after they had left for the evening! I deduced this pretty quickly when I was unable to drop off to sleep. I kept getting out of bed to smudge the house and myself, but there was simply too much energy left behind...I resolved my intention to journey for a simple ritual to clear and cleanse my living space after a large lodge...the spirits gave me a very easy prescription which involved nothing fancier than a broom and bowl of burning sage. Placing the bowl in the center of the room, I reached up with the broom to the four corners of the room, "sweeping" in circular motions, collecting the energies that tend to gravitate into corners, and shaking them off over the burning sage. While doing this, I was to speak these words: "May any energy that is not natural to this space transform into peace and harmony now. May all who reside in this dwelling live and sleep and dream in peace." I enacted this circular ritual in every room of the house where people had gathered, including the bathroom. It took less than 10 minutes and afterward I fell asleep easily, slept soundly and awakened refreshed and peaceful certain the house was cleared of other people's energetic debris.

O that this too too solid flesh would melt,
Thaw, and resolve itself into a dew!
Or that the Everlasting had not fix'd
His canon 'gainst self-slaughter! O God! O God!
How weary, stale, flat, and unprofitable
Seem to me all the uses of this world!
Fie on't! O fie! 'tis an unweeded garden,
That grows to seed; things rank and gross in nature
Possess it merely. That it should come to this!
     HAMLET Act 1, scene 2

Ups and Downs

On the preceding page, Mr. Hamlet realizes the difficulty in killing himself is that God has deemed self-slaughter to be a sin. And our Hamlet is a God fearing fellow. This confounds him, as he is truly struggling with who he is, the value of his life, what he brings, or could bring to the unsavory machinations of his duplicitous step Father, the new King of Denmark. Okay, my clients have not been quite so dramatic, on reflection. Mostly.

In my healing practice I have met all kinds of people. Many were desperate enough to consider, at least obliquely, putting an end to their misery. They all have one thing in common, they want to feel better! Some clients prefer that I together with my helping spirits do all the work, while they wait for a miracle cure. It is important to understand that while miracles do happen, cures take time; they require focus and attention from the clients themselves. Above all, they cannot prevent the possibility that new problems could occur later. Even the most dedicated self- healer is bound to bump up against life's ups and downs periodically.

The more we learn to take care of ourselves, the more we hope to sustain a feeling of good will, harmony and balance. It is inevitable, though, that eventually we will face a situation or crisis which will require us to marshal all our spiritual helpers and use all the tools in our spiritual tool kit to get through it. Life is difficult. Pain and loss do occur. Sometimes it seems as if nothing we try is helping. Sometimes we get so burdened and overwhelmed we get depressed. We feel unable to cope. This is far more common an occurrence than you can possibly imagine. If you have tried everything, if you have asked your friends for suggestions and tried those too, if you have done self-healing, gone for healings, and smelled every potentially helpful aroma, ingested every conceivably useful plant, burned every helping herb, sought the light of the Creator in your being, gone to sauna, sweated out your toxins, prayed, journeyed, meditated, performed Reiki, attended workshops, and so on, and you still feel miserable, there is one last thing you can do:

Help someone else! It's corny and cliché, but it works and it's good energy to share!

There was a particular time I fell into a black depression. The issue for me was around appreciation. I was substitute teaching part time while my healing practice was beginning to grow. The students I encountered at school were often hostile, resentful and frequently out of control. The urban school district had recently instituted what amounted to a pay cut for subs and I hadn't been given a raise in 7 years. I didn't have any covered benefits or health insurance from the district. The district didn't provide training and there were other substitute teachers whose inability to manage a classroom effectively had created the expectation on the part of students and administration alike that "subs" were second class, the lowest of the low, unimportant and not worthy of their respect. Other teachers often contributed to the problem by failing to leave updated seating charts or viable lesson plans during their absences. At work, I felt that I existed in a world where no one appreciated anything I did on their behalf. What made things even worse, I cared about my job and my students, investing energy and attention in providing them with their education although their regular teacher was absent. Frankly, the students seemed to prefer the "Do Nothing" subs who read their newspapers and left them alone. Sometimes I'd return from school and just cry, exhausted from my efforts to help students who had no interest in learning. I attempted to weave some of my spiritual tools into the school day. I quietly merged with my true self in the classroom. I put my symbol for Divinity on the chalkboard. I showed the students my compassion and empathy. I tried humor. I used different clearing techniques on myself throughout the day when I could find a moment. I told the students I didn't hold a grudge when they complained, "Why-dja get me into trouble?"

Unfortunately, nothing was working and I became depleted from all the negativity and hostility that was overtly directed at me, seemingly from all corners of the school. Because of my sensitive receptors it followed that even after school I was unable to shake all the dark energy that seemed to cling to me. Nothing in life gave me joy anymore, I felt worthless and hopeless.

What a terrible state! And even more devastating is the realization that so many of us go through periods of darkness like this. It is unfortunately fairly common.

During this time, I had been contacted by a potential new client. This gentleman of 38 had recently been the victim of a heart attack which would have been traumatic enough, but that was not why he contacted me. He explained that he felt he had no real personality, although he felt he used to have one when he was younger. He had been unable to feel "himself" for 20 years. I hauled myself out of the depths of my own despair to go to work to assist this fellow. He was the perfect client...He willingly followed every instruction, every ritual the spirits required of him...When we first began our work together, I did a soul retrieval for him in which I brought back three aspects of his vital essence, as well as a power animal. But other than a brief 30 minute period later on the day of the healing where he felt really himself and just great, he seemed to be right back where he started. In the following weeks I suggested to him that if he could feel good for 30 minutes, he could feel good again. I turned to my spirit helpers to see what more could be done. The client came back in two weeks. As I explained to him what steps we would take, and how they would differ from the previous healing, he stood and said to me, "Frannie, I want you to know how much I appreciate the way you are really trying to help me."

I almost cried. I told him, "You have no idea how much what you just said means to me right now." Then I went on to locate and extract the obstructions that blocked him from being able to feel his returned soul essence. I checked on his power animal and was told it was still very much with him, ready to help. I retrieved a beautiful rose hued shining sphere as a symbol of his authentic soul, and then checked to see if there was any soul essence that was now ready to be retrieved that hadn't been able to return in the earlier healing. I found his 14 year old self stuck deep in a well and it took many of my helpers to lift that essence out. Then it was very excited to come back to my client! I realized that this important piece had split off at a time when he was having adolescent identity issues, and without that piece he had been truly unable to feel himself…as if his identity had been arrested in adolescence. This last piece felt right, and I was glad indeed to return this to him. Before he left, I suggested we do a guided visualization to meet his true self. He warned me he wasn't able to visualize, so I suggested he just allow an inner knowing to transpire. At its conclusion, he was very excited and told me he had met himself, seen his own wisdom, and felt very positive indeed. A week or so later, he instant messaged me with the two most beautiful words: "Doing better."

My depression actually began to lift after our first session together. Although it took two sessions for him to finally find and feel himself as a whole, adult person, I knew from the start that, as they say, "Help was on the way." When he had earnestly told me how much he appreciated how hard I was trying to help him, I felt myself become whole again, just like that—through the magic of his appreciation.

Appreciation is everything. When all else fails, and depression has you in its grip, try to muster one last bit of motivation and find someone else to help. Somewhere there is someone who needs exactly what you can provide, and appreciation will place you on that path. I find that one heartfelt "Thank you" can compensate for months of disillusionment.

I practice being in appreciation wherever I go. This is an easy practice to incorporate into your life. The more you show appreciation, the more showing appreciation becomes a positive habit for you. Start your day by appreciating that you are alive! (Another morning ritual!) I get delighted when I see the look of startled pleasure on the face of someone—usually a stranger—when I say, "I appreciate what you did…who you are…what you said…how you said it…" There are myriad ways we can show appreciation to the other human bubbles swirling on our magic wands…appreciating others randomly as well as specifically… we can create a beautiful circle of appreciation to shimmer around ourselves, our homes, our communities…a glistening soap bubble cleansing our earth…*the more we appreciate life the softer, safer, saner, and sweeter the energy we leave in our passing…*

DUKE SENIOR:
Now, my co-mates and brothers in exile,
Hath not old custom made this life more sweet
Than that of painted pomp? Are not these woods
More free from peril than the envious court?
                    AS YOU LIKE IT, Act 2, Scene 1

HOLOFERNES:
This is a gift that I have, simple, simple; a foolish extravagant spirit, full of forms, figures, shapes, objects, ideas, apprehensions, motions, revolutions. These are begot in the ventricle of memory, nourished in the womb of pia mater, and delivered upon the mellowing of occasion. But the gift is good in those in whom it is acute, and I am thankful for it.
                    LOVE'S LABORS LOST, Act 4, Scene 2

The Sacred Circle

Much has been written about the power of the circle and this section is intended to awaken or increase awareness about this power. Fundamentally, each aspect of the circle is inherently connected to every other aspect of the same circle; it is a continuous whole without beginning or ending. In <u>Dreaming With The Wheel,</u> authors Sun Bear, Wabun, and Shawnodese wrote:

> The circle is one of the natural shapes of life and a central symbol for most Earth people. It represents life without beginning or ending, life that continues. The circle encompasses everything in the universe, from the entirety of the universe itself to the smallest microbe found within. Earth peoples respected the circle as they respected life. When they came together to counsel they sat in a circle. In much of their construction they reminded themselves of the circle, and of the continuous flow of life. Today, physics is finding that much of the energy of life is circular or spiraling.

It is no accident that wedding rings were chosen as the symbol of eternal commitment and devotion rather than something one pins on one's clothing, as one does with a medal. Because circles embrace the notion of infinity, they call up the essence of the Divine. Thus circles created with focus, intention, and awareness can become sacred places or objects where we can shift our energies into a tandem rhythm with a higher power.

Some historical examples of sacred circles include the monolithic stone circle at Stonehenge, the detailed Tibetan mandala paintings,

Medicine Wheels built of stones or other objects found in nature, the *Inipi*, or sweat lodge structure comprised of bent saplings, the bowl of the *Chanupa*—the sacred Pipe used in Native American prayer, and the ceremonial *kivas* of the Pueblo Indians. Many homes of indigenous people were constructed in circles, such as the grass covered dwellings of the Pacific Coast tribes, the *tipis* of the Plains Indians, the *hogans* of the Navajo and the *yurts* from Mongolia. Ancient circular labyrinths designed for meditation or contemplation are being rediscovered just as new ones are being constructed. There are protective circles which have been cast for vision quests and other earth-based ceremonial purposes; additionally, the Chinese art of Feng Shui teaches that *chi*, life force energy, flows more optimally in rooms that are set up to resemble circles. Energy moves more easily when not impeded by angles and corners. Let us not forget the ubiquitous crop circles, either.

A wonderful harmony in roundness, nature delivers to us the cycle of seasons, the cycles of our moon, sun and the planets in their orbits; our own 24 hour day is a circle. As you continue to consider sacred circles, you will probably find personal examples of how they work in your own life, and in the world around you. Wherever we find them, circles are symbols of completeness…and awareness of this can enrich our lives by making us feel more whole.

There is something spiritually potent permeating the energy inside a sacred circle. Sun Bear, an Ojibwa medicine man, described receiving a powerful vision in the late 1970s. He saw a wide circle of rocks that were placed like wheel spokes on a high hilltop. There was another, smaller circle of rocks placed inside the larger circle. A buffalo skull was inside the center circle. From all four directions came people donned in costumes that honored the totems of the animal kingdom. Sun Bear recognized this Sacred Circle as the hoop of his people when they entered it in a sun-wise direction and established their places on the wheel. He saw people from all the clans holding peace in their hearts. The Wheel was the crucible that created a linkage with the energies of the universe. As such, wise teachers would congregate there to share with the people and with each other. In the wise teachings of the stones and their animal, mineral or plant symbols, the nations could find healing, peace, harmony and a better world. Sun Bear's vision was that the imbalance in the world derived from the people themselves. In his vision, Sun Bear saw that the Sacred Medicine Wheel can teach the proper balance for peace between all nations, and respect for all of creation (Sun Bear xv, xvi).

The Bear Tribe, founded by Sun Bear, has sponsored Medicine Wheel Gatherings at which as many as a million people over time have danced around the wheels of stones. Wind Daughter, Chief of the Bear Tribe, is still bringing these wheels forward annually. My own tutelage with the Bear Tribe began in 1992 with an 11 day Vision Quest program, followed by an apprenticeship of several years during which time I became a Pipe Carrier, Water Pourer of the Sweat Lodge, and Ceremonialist. I attended numerous Medicine Wheel Gatherings and participated in ceremonies of building, awakening and empowering the Wheel. I have spent many hours with my own personal "dance" around the Wheel, learning from the wisdom of the 36 stones representing the elements, minerals, plants, animals, colors, seasons, time of day, time of life and clan groups. Each moment spent connected to the energies of the Medicine Wheel brought me into a deeper connection with my Creator, and with the earth and its abundant richness of knowledge. The voices of the gathered people lifted in chant and song connected the essence of my heart to theirs...friends and families were born, crafts were made and purchased, workshops led by a variety of Native American elders provided sustenance for the spirit; nothing could surpass the sheer power of hundreds of like-minded, spirit-minded people's hearts and souls joined together in common cause to lift all of our relations into beauty, blessing, and peace.

With proper focus and intention and awareness, we can ourselves learn to create and awaken the magical, healing properties of the sacred circle, whether we are planning a circle of stones, or pine cones, or twigs with feathers...any object found in nature that has been respectfully gathered can serve. Sun Bear's vision included 36 stones, each dedicated to a specific characteristic, e.g. "trust". A number other than 36 that has significance for you can be utilized, typically grouping in units of four. Each object should be chosen to represent the particular strengths you desire to awaken in your wheel (and soul). The clusters of four should include the cardinal directions. You can utilize four seasons, four types of healing, i.e., mental, emotional, spiritual and physical, the four races of humans, and so on. What is important is to make choices with an awareness of your impact on the earth and natural world. For example, if you are looking for stones or twigs in the woods, it is good to be cognizant that when you lift them up, you may be disturbing the eco-system of some smaller being, such as worms, ants, or other small creatures. The twigs you think will work so well may in fact be a part of some lair or habitat you are about to disturb. It is good to walk gently when you are looking for the building components of your Wheel, to pay attention to what kind of impact you create with your presence, with your footsteps. In the Bear Tribe, we offer a little organic tobacco or corn meal in appreciation for nature's gifts. With attention, you'll notice if a particular stone seems unwilling to be moved. If you need a crow bar to lift it, it might be best left where it is. It's good to quiet your mind, and awaken your inner eye to the subtle energies moving within and without you as you make your way through fields, woods, over hills, and streams. That bird call that keeps whistling in your ear may come from a location that has a gift for you… something for your Wheel…or something else for your spirit. You may want to review the section in this book on finding and building a relationship with a power spot to assist you in this endeavor.

Whatever materials you or your group use to create your sacred circle will be perfect just as you have chosen them—or maybe they have chosen you! As long as you approach your encounters in nature with focus, intention and awareness, come and go quietly with respect and appreciation, leave an offering…and open your heart to the subtle energies abounding, you will be able to build the circle of your own vision.

Use all of your senses to discern the right location for your circle or Wheel, if out of doors. If building a sacred space in your home or office, you may also want to spend some time quieting your mind and tuning in to where the circle wants to be placed…you can do a sage smudge of the area first, then listen with your inner knowing for the answer. You can create a circle that will last for decades or something that will last for an hour. In Shamanic communities, we usually sit in a circle, and community healings take place within the support of a circle of loving drummers, singers and other healers. The energy of the circle amplifies the healing power exponentially and bears witness to the transformation.

Once constructed, you should honor and awaken the sacred energies of the circle with the smudging of sage and especially the offering of tobacco or cornmeal. Speak a few focused prayers describing your purpose for the wheel. Call in the benevolent spirits of your location. Include the cardinal directional spirits. You will dedicate each individual component of your wheel. Use heartfelt words, rattle or drum; then, with purity of intention in your heart and awareness of all that you are doing—and all that you are receiving—you can enter into complete oneness with the very essence of all our relations. Thus the circle will awaken, enliven, empower, embrace, teach, hold, love, respect and honor *you* multifold in return for the energy you bring to *it*. In all, when you are inside the sacred circle you will have opportunity to shift your being on every level, into a deep connection with All That Is. From within this sacred space you can sing, dance, hum, tone, visualize, journey, meditate, draw, paint, write…if you can imagine it, you can create it. *A'bra K'dabra!* We connect ourselves from within our deepest essence to all that is around us. As within, so without. This is the way of it.

3rd GENTLEMAN:
At length her grace rose, and with modest paces
Came to the altar, where she kneel'd, and saint-like
Cast her fair eyes to heaven, and pray'd devoutly;
Then rose again and bow'd her to the people:
When by the archbishop of Canterbury
She had all the royal makings of a queen,
As holy oil, Edward Confessor's crown,
The rod, and bird of peace, and all such emblems
Laid nobly on her...
              HENRY THE EIGHTH Act 4, scene 1

Altars

Altars, like the circles we just read about, assist in manifesting spiritual energy and bringing that energy into ordinary reality. They are often places that focus attention on worship or ritual. They can become the center of focused prayer. I would describe a personal altar as a special place that is set aside inside or outside of your home, business or place of worship where certain significant items have been assembled mindfully and with purity of heart. The intention is that these items will receive your focused attention for the purpose of awakening the very energies the items on the altar symbolize. Altars can serve a variety of purposes including the following: There are altars for healing, those that honor ancestors, power animals and spiritual teachers, religious gods or deities such as Buddha, Ganesh, Jesus, Krishna, Kali, White Buffalo Woman, and so forth. There can be altars created to serve a specific purpose such as generating a better flow of income, honoring an intended outcome of a particular venture, or the manifestation of a love relationship. With creativity and imagination, one can create altars in various rooms in the home or garden.

Altars must be tended and given attention and energy for them to come alive. There are many ways to feed this energy: place rice, fruit or other food offerings, incense, crystals, candles, photos, flowers, seeds, totems and feathers are all useful in this context. We can also energize our altars by gazing at them as we walk by, or sit in contemplation. We can send Reiki energy, rattle, drum, sing and chant to awaken the energies.

Again, the idea is give *attention* with focused *intention*. With my clients I will frequently retrieve a power animal for them during a healing session. I tell them the best way to work with this power animal is to build a relationship. A good way to begin this relationship is to demonstrate your sincerity for friendship by creating a simple altar. Any space you designate as special will work to create an altar in your home. You can clear a shelf, or set up a small table. It can be energizing to drape a beautiful cloth on which to put the items you have assembled, which will be unique to your specific purpose. As ever, you can smudge your items with sage to purify them. *The number of items you place is less important than the intent with which you choose and place them.*

I like to sit and regard the objects, drinking in their symbolism and power, thinking about what they mean to me and listening to any messages I hear…I also love the large altars that are created in large workshops or healing circles. It is beautiful to see what many diverse people bring to place on the altar for a blessing. The energy in the room grows as each person adds their item. The altar gathers strength from the group. A medicine wheel is also an altar. It is wise to be respectful and honor what is placed there by approaching from a place of humility.

I have written a lot about spirits, power and energy…these are not words I'm bandying about …Life is about our energy and how we harness it. Where we put our attention is absolutely where our energy will follow. Thus with altars as with everything we do when we lead a conscious life, we must take the time to open our hearts and dream into what we want to honor…relax and breathe into what feels correct to us…then, with focused intent, with sacred herbs of sage, cedar, or essential oils such as lavender or myrrh, we are participating in the creation of what we wish to see manifest in our lives.

One must always manifest for the highest good, remembering the old adage that 'what goes around comes around'.

ROMEO:
If I profane with my unworthiest hand
This holy shrine, the gentle sin is this,
My lips, two blushing pilgrims, ready stand
To smooth that rough touch with a tender kiss.

JULIET:
Good pilgrim, you do wrong your hand too much,
Which mannerly devotion shows in this,
For saints have hands that pilgrims' hands do touch,
And palm to palm is holy palmers' kiss.
               ROMEO AND JULIET, Act 1, Scene 5

Touch Barriers

The most tangible form of connecting with another human being is through a shared touch. A firm handshake says, "I'm in this moment with you. Let's get down to business." A gently laid hand upon the shoulder can impart volumes of moral support; hands extended across a dinner table, or fingers intertwined, can end a fight, bridge a gap, or cement a proposal.

Babies crave touch. Many infants who fail to thrive despite adequate food or shelter are said to do so because they lack the comfort and safety of a loving human touch. In nursing homes otherwise functioning and recovering elderly patients can succumb to loneliness and despair because they lack the most basic life experience, being touched by another with compassion and love.

I came across a reality show on television about women dating in San Francisco several years ago. A reference was made to what they called "breaking the touch barrier". I interpret this to mean reaching across the isolation that separates men and women, and making a connective statement that implies, "I see you, hear you, and by touching you I acknowledge that I am available to enter into a conversation with you. I accept your energy and presence. I care."

In my darkest hours of despair, I know that what I most crave is to be held tenderly and lovingly; to have someone brush away my tears and kiss my fingertips. If this occurs, it is like a magic elixir and I become restored to balance very quickly.

Touching reminds us of our humanity, directs our moral compass and invites us to participate in the great well spring of love and connection that tantalizes us from every direction…a day trip to a shopping mall and a little observation will underscore this: We notice the elderly couple trying to balance packages and canes. She looks burdened, tired and perhaps in physical pain and he lightens her load by taking one of her bags...she smiles gratefully. He pats her hand, tucking it into the crook of his elbow in an old fashioned and courtly gesture. We understand how they have withstood the onslaught of 50 years together. Over by the fountain, a little boy walks its perimeter carefully, trailing his fingertips in the arc of splashing water droplets. From a safe distance, his mother watches him vigilantly. He trips and lands on his bottom in the fountain itself; surprised by the fall and becoming drenched, he bursts into angry tears. Mom is there in less than a heartbeat. She scoops him up and cradles him to her bosom. He tucks his head under her chin and after a few whimpers, his tears subside. In the shelter of Mom's protective touch, his world—so recently awry—is righted and he visibly relaxes. We see the teen age couple having soft drinks at the Food Court. They hold hands and talk quietly, in awe and wonder at the magic they are generating. It is powerful to see humans come together to share their commonality. Connecting their lives for a moment, an hour, or decades...

Still, innocent touches have fallen victim to a society in part comprised of real dangers: scary predators, child molesters, con artists, rapists, and muggers do walk our streets and frequent our regular haunts. In our busy, hustling world it can sometimes be a real challenge to touch or be touched safely. *It is essential to respect the physical boundaries of other people.*

In my Acting classes, I taught my students something which always caused great mirth called, "The 16 Inch Thing"...Culturally, Americans possess a comfort zone of a radius of about 16 inches around their bodies. For acting purposes, this was relevant because two characters can show the nature of their relationship to an audience without saying any words, merely by how close or far they stand within the 16 inch boundaries. Additionally, the kind of touch that is or is not exhibited can indicate the true nature of a relationship, whether work related, family oriented, friend or foe. Viola Spolin, author of Improvisation For the Theater, tells us that relationships can be communicated nonverbally by showing relationship through the physical expressions demonstrated between the actors as well as their proximity to each other in the scene. Our teenage couple at the mall broke the "touch barrier" and held hands intimately across the table. Without knowing their story, we see they are in love. Our elderly couple showed us their history, and their loving, protective concern for each other.

Negative touches are unwelcome, and today people are on guard against them. Two men engaged in pugilistic posturing circle and spar, moving in and out of close proximity, daring each other to see which of them will throw the first punch. In the public schools, teachers are routinely admonished not to touch their students, for it can so easily be misinterpreted. Yet most teachers do know the value of a literal pat on the back, a non-verbal, "Atta boy!"

We must be ever cognizant of the rules and mores of the society in which we live regarding protection from improper use of touch; yet, we must not forget that a simple human touch on the hand can easily convey what most of us so desperately crave: the feeling that we are not alone, that someone cares, that we are part of something good and safe and whole.

BOTTOM:
The Woosel cock so black of hue,
With orange tawny bill,
The Throstle with his note so true,
The Wren with little quill—
The Finch, The Sparrow, and the Lark,
The plain-song Cuckoo grey,
Whose note full many a man doth mark,
And dares not answer nay.
                   A MIDSUMMER NIGHT'S DREAM, Act Three,
          Scene one

Natural Talents

One of the saddest realities of modern life is that our sense of disconnection from ourselves often precludes us from truly connecting with our natural talents and the deepest yearnings of our soul. Consider the common obstacles: Societal expectations, the "good intentions" of family and friends, a teacher's unexpected rebuke, or the competing responsibilities of job and children, to name a few, can conspire to prevent us from fully attuning to our highest callings. Yet life is so precious and brief. Our time on this earth is certainly limited. Shouldn't we utilize our innate talents while we are here? There is only one answer to this question. YES!

I invite you to think about these questions:

1. What did you want to be when you grew up?

2. What were your secret—or not so secret—dreams for yourself?

3. Did you ever want to be a writer, dancer, singer, actor, gardener, chef, designer, doctor, midwife, architect, poet, teacher, financial wizard, politician, professional student, peace officer, balloon pilot, sky diver, adventurer, mountain climber, yogi, hermit, naturalist, musician….?.

4. Take a moment now to list 3-5 dreams or goals you may have once had or still have for yourself that you have not yet accomplished… any surprises?

5. If you have ever tried to accomplish any of these dreams, what kind of feedback did you get from family? From friends? From professionals in that field? From yourself? Was the feedback helpful or hurtful?

6. What do you think it would take for you to actualize one or more of your deferred dreams? Time? Money? Motivation? Encouragement?

Confidence? Take a moment now to list 3-5 actions you could take to begin to actualize your dreams. While you do this, take your own creative potential seriously (Cameron 34). No self-mocking, okay? Remember these admonitions:

- Listen and see with your heart.
- Forget being sensible for a while.
- You do deserve to explore your dreams.
- Those aren't real reasons to defer your dreams. (You know).
- It's your divine right to shine. Your Creator expects that of you in exchange for your being alive.
- Be your truest self and have a remarkable ride.

My experience is that dreams tend to get thrown onto dry dock because of the twin pronged evils of fear and inertia. Fear prohibits self-expression, and inertia prevents our giving attention to our dreams. When we live a life in which we are truly connected to our authentic selves, it becomes increasingly frustrating to ignore aspects of our potentials or desires that we intrinsically feel should be developed. Still, around us we do see people who have made the leap from "maybe someday" to "right now!" I remember once watching "Last Comic Standing" on television and there was this woman well past her prime, who had decided late in life to pursue her dream of stand-up comedy after being a homemaker. Michelle B. had been selected to participate in this program from literally hundreds of those who auditioned, and was wowing audiences with her delightful timing and droll wit. John Grisham, popular author of legal thrillers, left a life of practicing law to become a block buster writer. Do you think when he wrote his first book, A Time to Kill, that he knew how successful it would be? Al Gore, locked out of the presidency in 2000 by the U. S. Supreme Court, had to give up his lifelong dream of being our Commander in Chief; instead, he returned to his earlier dream of awakening people to the perils of global warming, and the need for action as he crisscrossed the globe giving his power point presentation, which ultimately became the documentary film, "An Inconvenient Truth", and led to a Nobel prize.

The Tao Te Ching freely explores how following the precepts of the Tao can support, expand and revitalize the writing process (Wahlstrom

102). These precepts can be applied to accomplishing any of your dreams. The idea is to prepare for a major goal while it is still small enough to manage and plan. In this way, difficult endeavors can be accomplished simply by breaking your project down into smaller steps. Thus the ubiquitous journey of a thousand miles that begins with a single step is the way of the Tao, the way of your dreams (verses 48, 64)

Look at your recently created list of hopes deferred. Can you narrow it down to one dream for now? You can do this through a number of methods. Journey, or meditate or ask for the answer to come to you in a dream at bed time. You can also employ the technique of automatic writing in which you write a question then use your opposite hand from the one you typically use to write the answer. You can also try a free association writing exercise: Brainstorm everything you can think of about your dream, your fears, hopes, what has been limiting you, what might inspire you, who might support you, whose advice you should seek, and so forth and write it all down without censoring.

Once you have narrowed your list down to the dream that will most activate your soul, you must then ask yourself the single most important question: *What must I do first to turn this dream into becoming a reality?* Perhaps the first thing you must do is to say it out loud! I believe that where we focus our attention is where our energy goes. I recommend writing and posting your intention to manifest your dream on your mirror or somewhere you will see it daily, as a reminder! It is important to cull through all the old ideas you've harbored around this dream, for they haven't served you well. If they would have, your dream would already be manifest in this world! While it is important to have support and the encouragement of like-minded people to assist you on your path, it is also necessary to weed out those people who have nothing positive to contribute to your effort.

This is a tale of how I let another person undermine my dream. When I was 24, I decided to write a novel. As most first efforts go, it was fairly auto-biographical. My intention was to spend the summer of 1979 writing this book. Today it would be an example of early "Chick Lit" before that genre had been so named. That was the summer of 1979 when I left New York and traveled around the country, with my old electric typewriter and big brown folder, I wrote in my sister's kitchen in Madison, Wisconsin, at a Best Western in Hannibal, Missouri, and other places. People I met along the way heard that I was writing a book and seemed interested and enthusiastic. I wrote over 125 pages before I made it to New Orleans to visit an old high school chum of mine who was finishing up his residency at Tulane University. He offered to read what I wrote. With confidence and pride I turned over my manuscript. After he finished reading (however much he actually read) he said, "Stick to acting, Fran". This comment utterly devastated my confidence. I never wrote another word of that book. All my excitement, desire and focus had turned to chalk in my throat when I heard those words. People who we admire, friends and family who profess to have our best interests at heart, can exact serious sabotage on our dreams. So while it is essential to have a support group in place, it is even more critical to choose your supporters very carefully. Constructive criticism is useful only if it comes from a place of genuine caring. We need the kind of feedback that will alert us to missteps without crushing our egos and dreams in the process.

My biggest fear around the writing of this book was that no one would think I had anything particularly significant to say, or else that it has all been said before, so why bother? Even when I had begun the process of writing it, I doubted its relevancy. Initiated the summer I hurt my foot and was laid up, it mostly languished over the following winter. Eventually, I mustered up the courage to email a few of the essays that are now incorporated into this text. I chose them carefully. First, I sent a doctor I knew the section on Medical Disconnection, which I figured he'd read with interest as he is a holistic physician and chiropractor. I also sent him the section on hugging a tree. His feedback was short and quick: "I liked it. It was well written." Two sentences in one breath, made up for "Stick to acting, Fran." Unfortunately, almost 30 years have intervened between these two reactions; so, again, choose your supporters carefully!! You don't want someone who will kill your ideas out of hand, but you don't need someone who will just love all your ideas, either. You want someone who will honestly and fairly assess your steps and make suggestions that will further enable you to accomplish your goals and dreams! Someone who will pick it apart without offering anything positive is someone to avoid if at all possible.

Connecting to one's lost dreams can revitalize and enrich your life in unexpected ways. There are many ways to fulfill one's dreams. For example, if you've always wanted to sing but don't have "American Idol" aspirations, you can find a local choir, religious or secular. If you've always wanted to play guitar, but don't see yourself living the rock 'n roll life, you can volunteer to play your music at a nursing home or homeless shelter.

The full experience of something can often be realized in very small ways. When I had my first acting contract at the Barn Dinner Theater in Roanoke, Virginia, people from the audience would come knocking on my dressing room door at intermission. Friends and family sent flowers and telegrams. It was small scale, but I figured out pretty quickly that the experience of being paid and having fan support was already upon me, the only difference over time would be the volume and intensity. If we stay alert to the subtle nuances, we may discover it is substantially easier to live out our dreams than we had first imagined. This is not to say you should give up on being famous! Just recognize that the lesson or experience can also be quiet, yet still fulfilling. Sometimes we can fully assimilate a life experience and integrally know that the moment has been plumbed for its essence. Then we have freed our soul to accomplish whatever it is that our soul craves next. I'm all for feeding the soul!

MACBETH:
Tomorrow, and tomorrow, and tomorrow,
Creeps in this petty pace from day to day,
To the last syllable of recorded time;
And all our yesterdays have lighted fools
The way to dusty death. Out, out, brief candle!
Life's but a walking shadow, a poor player,
That struts and frets his hour upon the stage,
And then is heard no more. It is a tale
Told by an idiot, full of sound and fury,
Signifying nothing.
                MACBETH, Act 5, scene 3

Disappointment

I have to smile wryly as I set out to begin this chapter. My lovely, cushiony swivel desk chair broke the other day (with me in it!), thus I'm currently perched on a stationary, straight Amish ladder back—one of two left from a set of eight that were burned in my 1995 house fire. It's 95 degrees outside, and the only working air conditioner is in my son's old room; its chill does not spread to my work space.

Disappointment....was there ever time for such a word? Ah, the myriad ways in which life can disappoint us never cease to surprise, amaze, and—well—disappoint. Aside from the broken chair and rivulets of sweat running down my chest, I spent the morning going over bills and statements with the unhappy conclusion that I will be out of living funds quite shortly should something miraculous not occur tout de suite. My aging mother is suffering from an excruciating gout attack which requires my devoted time and attention, and my garden is languishing under the hot, dry sun despite my fervent efforts to water early this morning. My 12 year old cat Bonita suddenly has a thyroid condition that causes her to drastically lose weight unless I administer medication twice a day. The brother cats, Yarrow and Angelo alternate between disappointing rounds of spraying and inappropriate urination. Argh!!

Then again, if I take just a moment to look at the flip side, I see that the broken chair can also symbolize the final end to a life-long, disappointing, relationship with a youthful amour from my girlhood, who, in fact, had gifted me the chair in the first place. With the old boyfriend chair gone, I can clear his lingering resonance from my soul and create more space for a partner that is more than a memory.

I was surprised by the unexpected silver lining that came alongside our traumatic yet transforming house fire in 1995; it jettisoned me into setting down roots on my land here, and constructing the sweat lodge. While I think I will forever miss my wedding crystal, smashed into the rubble of what was my post fire kitchen, I do like the Amish country table and hutch that replaced my old oak pedestal table, which turned to charcoal from the fire, as well. I have faith that money will find its way to me soon. My mother's gout will pass in due time, Bonita will heal, and eventually it WILL rain. I'm a bit less optimistic about the peeing cats, but we must retain some disappointment and frustration or life would just be boring. (How pungent it is...we can always rely on cat urine to motivate us into action!)

Meanwhile, the more common scenario is that for most of us disappointments tend to pile up. Bubbles do periodically burst. Setbacks get in the way of forward momentum, and getting a good night's sleep, to say the least. Thus we must focus our energies and give them their due attention before we can begin to transmute them into something positive.

I once knew an Army captain, hardened by a career in the military and two tours of duty in Viet Nam. He was fond of exhorting: "No expectations, no disappointments". Truer words have not been spoken. When we project our views of desired outcomes onto the situations or people whom we encounter, we tend to cling to those views, and that tenacity prevents us from being in the here and now. If we can sustain the ability to stay truly present in the actual moment, without projecting what should happen on to the next moment, then when the next moment comes, we are more prepared to meet it with an open mind and open heart. Essentially, what it boils down to is this: The more open we remain, the less disappointed we become.

The Buddhist approach embraces the concept of non-attachment. They have an interesting idea about people, and how they appear in our lives. It is said that everyone in your life is a friend, a foe, or a stranger to you. The caution here is to remember that these three variations of human relationship undergo continual ebb and flow. Sometimes the sands shift out from under us; other times the tides bring new adventures or people to us. The friend today can be tomorrow's foe; today's stranger can be tomorrow's lover, and so forth. The man who gifted me with this now deceased desk chair was once a friend, then he became a lover. Now he is a stranger. Wouldn't it be interesting if he was reading this very chapter at this very moment? If he is, can I have a new chair?

Okay, I hear my Readers crying, we get it, we get it...but what if who we are disappointed in is *ourselves*? Ah. That one really hurts, right? If you disappoint me, I can say, okay, not your fault, I saw the danger and I hurtled toward it. I'm at fault. I should have seen the signs...I should have heard the coldness in his voice....I shouldn't have made that left turn, signed that contract, gotten that speeding ticket, eaten that potato salad at the picnic....Has anyone figured out the antidote to all this self-negativity? If you guessed *self-forgiveness,* you hit it on the head. If you guessed something else, please write to me so I can try it too!

Perhaps the single clearest facet in becoming a mature individual is the ability to forgive oneself for one's transgressions, whatever they are. We are truly spiritual beings having a material experience, and it is imperative for our health to shed our shame, guilt, and negative self-talk. The more we dwell on what has gone wrong, what we did wrong, and how much we are to blame, then the less we are able to focus on creating new and positive outcomes. We can do what will be right. We can alter things for the good. This is not to say that I'm encouraging you to skip all self-analysis, not at all, as you will see in the following.

Exercise for Shifting Disappointment Energy/Automatic Writing

Before you begin this, it is helpful for you to sit quietly and calm your mind with your breath. you will need pen and paper. Relax into your chair or pillows, or lean gently against a tree trunk. Inhale deeply through your nose, and exhale slowly through your mouth for several minutes. Pay particular attention to the exhale...when you are relaxed and your mind has quieted, allow yourself to focus your attention onto those matters that disappoint you at the present time. Next allow yourself to examine your role in those matters...allow the thoughts to enter and exit your mind without grasping any one of them other than to quickly jot down a note to remind you later what it was. While you are in this peaceful and reflective state of mind, let your body wander and move—out of doors into nature if possible. As you focus your attention on your disappointment, notice if you can feel any changes in your body that accompany the changes in your thought. Sometimes we constrict certain muscles—particularly in our backs or necks—when we are disappointed. See if you can gently loosen or release physical tension by alternately tensing and relaxing the constricted places in your body. If you are outside, find a tree, flower, rock, or river where you can bring these questions to the nature spirits:

- What is it that I was expecting?
- What have I not received?
- What is it that MOST disappoints me?
- What can I bring to bear on this matter that will result in a sense of "enough"?
- How can I shift my energy to feel satisfied with "what it is" and with "who I am"?

Make yourself comfortable in the natural setting you have chosen with your notes from before and write your questions one at a time. Do this even if you previously jotted them down. In the space where the answer should be, use your *opposite* hand (left if you are right handed, etc.) and holding your pen, let your unconscious guide you to the answers you seek. As the information comes to you, write it down. This is called automatic writing. By using the opposite hand you release the blockages that constrict the open heart and mind and allow the spirit to flow. If you are someone who is generally open to subtle energies, you may be able to hear directly, otherwise the automatic writing will help to shift your awareness. These questions would all make for interesting shamanic journeys, for those of you who are shamanic practitioners as well. Regardless of the approach you take, remember to clearly state your intentions, and to ask only one question at a time, receiving your answers before moving to the next journey, or the next question.

When we connect to the existentialism of disappointment, we are at last in that place of no place, what is called *shunyata* in Buddhism, and *b'leemah* in Hebrew; the place of emptiness, the void. From here we can view the past flow of events with eagle precision, and thus can allow ourselves to see the moment the disappointment began, and from within that emptiness just before that moment, we can allow ourselves to feel fully forgiven. We can also become forgiving and reveal the best qualities of human nature.

When we visit nature spirits for guidance and assistance, we then allow ourselves to connect deeply and soulfully with our own authenticity.

Like as the waves make towards the pebbled shore,
So do our minutes hasten to their end;
Each changing place with that which goes before,
In sequent toil all forwards do contend.
Nativity, once in the main of light,
Crawls to maturity, wherewith being crown'd,
Crooked eclipses 'gainst his glory fight,
And Time that gave doth now his gift confound.
Time doth transfix the flourish set on youth
And delves the parallels in beauty's brow,
Feeds on the rarities of nature's truth,
And nothing stands but for his scythe to mow:
And yet to times in hope my verse shall stand,
Praising thy worth, despite his cruel hand.
              SONNET 60

Time

We enter this world with an unspecified but finite allotment of time. Time is our gift from our Creator, and it is our human birthright—even obligation to use this span of years productively, creatively, and consciously. I recall the words from Ecclesiastes 3-1: "To everything there is a season, a time for every purpose under heaven". The choices we make as to how we spend our time inform the course of our lives, season after season.

The seasons of passing time reflect the stages of a human life, i.e., childhood, adolescence, educational pursuits, parenting, work, play, maturation, and the sunset years. When our time is up, and we prepare to exit this "mortal coil", will we be able to say, "I used my time as best I could to accomplish as much as I was meant to do in this world? Did I create something of lasting value? Was I a decent human being? Did I give back? Did I respect the gift that it is to be a spiritual being in a human body? Did I respect who it is that I am? Did I choose to use my time wisely (for me), or did I fall into societal expectations and just shuffle along with the groundlings, hoping it would all be for the best in the end?"

These are the questions to ponder. For me, life is an endless exploration of what is around the next bend. I have honestly resisted life's attempts to restrict my boundaries, and have literally pulled and tugged and yanked off the shackles of "should-ness". When I found myself stuck back in Michigan after one year studying acting in Boston, I chafed at the limitation, threw off the yoke, and moved to New York, the better to pursue my dreams at that time. When my acting pursuits took me to the dinner theatre circuit in Texas, eventually I chafed at the creative limitations of that experience, and followed my urge to do more substantial theatre work, ultimately seasoning as an acting teacher and director. Years later, I turned a lay off from a "should" job as a marketer into a trip to South Korea, which then turned into a marriage. When I was pregnant overseas, I campaigned for two years to convince my husband that it was the right choice to come back to the States and raise our child in freedom and security. How grateful I was to be living at home in the good old U S of A when our complicated divorce began.

With divorce came the shattering of our family security and it seemed that everyone told me I would have to relinquish my dream of raising my son myself. They recommended I search for full time employment, since I would be raising him without benefit of his father in the home. I just kept reminding myself that I have a hand in the creation of my life. It wasn't always easy to persevere with my choice to be a full time mom especially when it meant more of a struggle financially. There was much I personally did without, but overall I managed to provide my son with a stable, loving, enriched and supportive childhood. I carefully evaluated how I used my time. I weighed the cost of working against paying other people to do what I could be doing if I wasn't working full time. As I considered how to create and build a future for myself and my son, who was quite young at the time, I discovered an easier lifestyle when one ascribed to a philosophy of *voluntary simplicity*. These words became my credo, and I share them here with you now. "Simple living is about living deliberately. Simple living is not about austerity, or frugality, or income level. It's about being fully aware of why you are living your particular life, and knowing that life is one you have chosen thoughtfully. Simple living is about designing our lives to coincide with our ideals" (Luhrs).

Naysayers—"*You can't*"– "*You shouldn't*"– "*No one does that!*"–abound at every turn and opportunity…thus I put forth the proposition that there is enough time to live in our authenticity, if only we will support our own initiatives and courageously push through the naysayers to find the truth of what is the best way to live our own lives, one day at a time.

While I enjoyed my fruitful years teaching theatre and English in a Michigan high school, I did not enjoy the physical distance of the commute, and the excessive limitations on my parenting time. Additionally, I had to juggle my son's visitation schedule with his father as well as an intensely busy rehearsal schedule at school. I made choices that precluded meeting my immediate needs as I put the needs of my son, and the requirements of his childhood to the fore. As a consequence, when he reached middle school, and the latch-key option of childcare was no longer available, I negotiated a reduction in my time commitment at school; I relinquished teaching one class. This allowed me to start the school day slightly later, but late enough to get my son off to school myself; it did result in a decrease in my health insurance coverage, and the difference in the number of research papers to correct was only negligible, and I took a huge pay cut. After that I was available to start my son's day with organization, a home-made lunch, and see him off with a kiss and hug.

How we choose to spend our time is a direct result of where we put the focus of our attention. The energy follows the attention. It is always thus.

EXERCISE FOR CLARITY: Take out a piece of paper and itemize how you actually spend your time on an average day. Include every routine item, and typical activity. Do not edit, just write it all down, whatever it is—or isn't– applying cosmetics, shaving, driving, shopping, working –get it all down there. Next, put that paper aside (don't read it over yet). On a clean sheet of paper (oh, the possibilities of a clean sheet of paper!), write down what you would do on an average day if only you *took* the time. Again, do not censor yourself, just let your brain respond to the question and write whatever comes up. Now, put that paper aside, and go and do something else wisely with your time… Allow this exercise to percolate inside you. Notice if your mind drifts back to any of the items on either list; notice if you can sense any of your attachments to your lists shifting. The point of this exercise isn't for you to have an "Aha!" moment about how you do spend your time, *the point of this exercise is for you to discern how you WOULD spend your time, if only you could.*

Making changes in the way you allocate your time will come naturally once you can determine how you would spend your time, if only you could. Because *how* you would spend your time is the *voice of your soul* calling to you beyond years of social conditioning. Listen to that voice.

One thing is certain, I am not always a great model for time usage. I am subject to deep procrastination, and am forever juggling the importance of the items on my "to-do" lists. This very book is now 8 years since its inception, and I have myriad excuses for this delay, for the months and years where I wrote and edited almost nothing. Since this book began, my life has shifted in many ways: by choice, or by circumstance. Either way, one must react to the events, or plan for changes. At this moment, I finally have the time, but that doesn't always find me utilizing it appropriately, or creatively. It is precisely because I am so often squandering my own time that I am able to recognize how much richer life is when I am motivated, and filled with purpose, and living a time-conscious life.

Life unfolds, and our human role is a process revealing itself to us when our hearts and minds are open. We can make of it what we choose. Despite negative circumstances, guilt or shame, loss or sorrow, jealousy or hostility, joy and elation, times of plenty, and times of lean…we CAN make of it what we choose. The trick is to arrive clearly at an understanding of just what it is that speaks to our soul, that calls to us from the depths with a quiet insistency….hear this, feel this…do this…and then gather our energy to make it manifest.

Living consciously and authentically isn't just for a few. For all of us it is our deepest responsibility to live out of gratitude and respect for the gift of our seven or so decades as human beings alive on this beautiful earth. In fact, I would argue that this is our most important purpose.

DOCTOR:
No more be done:
We should profane the service of the dead
To sing a requiem and such rest to her
As to peace-parted souls.
Lay her i' th' earth,
And from her fair and unpolluted flesh
May violets spring! I tell thee, churlish priest,
A minist'ring angel shall my sister be
When thou liest howling.
                    HAMLET Act 5, scene 1

Death

It could be said that death is the ultimate disconnection. It certainly felt that way when my parents passed away within eight months of each other. My siblings and I had sometimes spoken about what life would be like when our parents were deceased. How would it feel to be ultimately cut off from them? Those 'what if conversations never approached what it actually was like to lose one of them when Dad passed away first. Unexpectedly, his death brought me much closer to my father than I ever was in life.

My Dad and I weren't affectionate, though I certainly tried. I was never a Daddy's Girl, and I remember more harshness and judgment than I do affection and support. A "man's man", my father loved to tinker with engines and build things. As a child, I loved going down into the basement to visit him in his workshop. The smell of sawdust can still take me back. He was also known as the "tractor doctor" and he rebuilt riding mowers for a hobby. In my mind he could fix anything mechanical, and I was excited to show him I could as well. When my sister and I quarreled over whose turn it was to have the AM/FM radio in their bedroom, Dad just took it away, and put it in his workshop to put an end to our sniping. I sneaked into the basement and sought the radio, discovering to my great dismay, that he had actually taken it apart (the better to prevent either of his daughters from enjoying it). Somehow, someway, I figured out how to put it back together until it worked. I was so proud! I carried it upstairs to my bedroom and plugged it in.

Dad never said one word to me about the radio, nor did he take it away. From that day forward it was mine, and only mine. Guess he figured I'd earned it. The larger, sadder lesson here was the way my

Dad parented: through denial and aggression. Dad was about what he didn't provide, more than what he did.

But, he was Dad. The only one. My siblings and I struggled for his love, and competed for his affection, but none of us got it anyway. He was a tough nut to crack; he survived his Mom's suicide when he was 6, remained perennially damaged, and took that out on us. Years later we would wonder to each other: what will it be like when he dies? Relief? Or even more loss, since the battle for his affection could no longer be waged?

Then the day came when we found out. Of course it was horrible, I can't say it wasn't. I got the early morning phone call from the hospital, where my 88 year old, once indomitable, father was lying unconscious with kidney and system failure. They wanted to know, "Does he have a DNR?" He did, and after talking to my out of state siblings on the phone, it was determined that he would be taken off life support, which was what he wanted. Now *that* was a stressful decision.

The staff in ICU was very caring; that didn't make it any less awful. I stood by Dad's head and whispered to him, "I forgive you. Go with love. Go to your parents. They are waiting for you. Go with love." I said the words, over and over, until he transitioned. Then he was gone. And I was suddenly achingly bereft, missing what I'd never known—being the recipient of my father's love. Did I forgive him? Who knew? He was gone, it didn't matter anymore.

Dad had always been adamant that he didn't want a funeral; his body was left to the Wayne State University Medical School in Detroit, Michigan for study. I had told him when he was still living that we were definitely going to have some kind of memorial service when he passed though he'd insisted he didn't want it. "It's for us, Dad. You can't deny us this."

I was creating a photographic memory board for the memorial service. By now, I was taking care of my Mom on a daily basis. She was suffering from Alzheimer's and MERSA among a plethora of dangerous medical ailments. I poked around her apartment looking for her old photos which she insisted I could not keep, and she must have returned. This was remarkable considering my mother had taken to her sickbed and not really emerged for the better part of a year at this point.

What I experienced during the creation of the memory board was nothing short of phenomenally healing. It took me a week. I sorted through decades of photos, trying to tell the story of his life: son of immigrants, who was raised by an emotionally distant stepmother, meeting my mom, the army, moving to Michigan and an administrative job at United Hebrew Schools, having a family, fixing tractors, building a cottage in the country. As I connected with my father's life story, I began to see it in HIS terms, instead of mine. Previously, my emotional life viz-a-viz my father, had always been about what I had lost, what he hadn't given to me. But now, in black and white, and sometimes color, was his life arranged on that board chronologically, and I could see that the fathering part of his life was really only a small chunk of it. It sort of blew my mind. I gained this great perspective and felt oddly better. Somehow, being able to visualize the whole span of his life helped bring me some solace about the difficult times I'd had with him. Children tend to think, "It's all about me.", and for a while it is. He was still gone, but I was able to understand that despite what I'd lost or never had from him, I was just a blip on his radar screen despite the fact that he'd haunted my own emotional life for decades.

The intensity of my grief surprised me. I doubled up in tears on the floor. The dream was dead. The dream that I could one day matter to a man who would love and cherish and appreciate me was dead. Long live the dream.

Life goes on, it really does. One gets up in the morning, writes a eulogy, plans a memorial service...people come to support you and then...it's time to move on. Partly because Dad's presence in my life was more in my head than in reality. I didn't miss seeing him much, because I hadn't heard much from him to tell the truth. The biggest surprise, however, came when I began talking to him when I was trying to do something mechanical, accomplish a home repair, or work on the mower. I spoke out loud and asked him to show me what to do in order to help me figure out the next step. Sometimes I'd get information flooding my brain and was just stunned that it was there. I still do this, call on him to show me how to fix something. In these moments, when I get this flooding of awareness, of "Aha!" when I'm trying to fix something, I feel deeply connected to him. Not to whom I wanted him to be, not to the man whose love I couldn't capture. I felt connected to his essence. To *him*.

There is freedom in putting down the struggle. I learned that forever he would not love me as I'd wished. Yet instead of that being a sore wound, I began to feel the wound closing. I found the courage to end the relationship I was in, in which I was repeating the same endless struggle for love and attention. I figured, hey, if I'm not getting it from Dad ever, I'm sure not going to struggle for it with this guy anymore.

Eight months later, Mom passed away, leaving big blanks in my life. Mom and I had been close, and I had been her primary caregiver, essentially running her apartment as an assisted living center; managing her meds, her meals, her doctor appointments, her hospitalizations, nursing home stays, finances, etc. It had become a full time job—keeping her alive.

She had the kind of death no one wants for their loved one—she suffered—and terribly—and for an extremely long time. I was helpless, although I tried everything to help her. I became an expert on her medical conditions and could rattle off prescriptions, side effects, and medical procedures. I spent so much time in hospitals and nursing homes the staff in these places often assumed I was a health care worker. I gave her healing herbal tea, learned about a supplement that ended her painful, chronic bouts with gout, and cooked healthy meals which she picked at to please me. I arranged for a massage therapist to come to her home. I managed the aides that came to assist (a full time job in itself). Despite my loving ministrations, Mom continued to spiral down. I think she was ready for her death long before I was ready to accept that she wanted to be done.

The sense of disconnection I experienced after Mom passed was much more intense than with Dad. This made sense as we'd spent so much time together, especially the last two years while she was slowly dying. The last cogent thing my mother said to me from her death bed, at home in her hospice setting, was, "Go home. I want you to have a life." She lived perhaps one week longer but never spoke coherently to me again.

Within hours of her transition, my sister and I washed and dressed her body. I put lavender oil on her chakras. One last time I climbed into bed with her, and my heart flooded. One last time my tears touched her cheeks.

The last physical connection I had with my mother was at the viewing, at the funeral home. Although we had asked the undertakers not to fuss with her hair, they had styled it in some ridiculous "do". A very peculiar shade of lipstick was on her mouth. She looked nothing like my mother. They had made her unrecognizable and I was furious. I stood next to her in her white shroud, fretting about the absurd hair and make-up and knew my mother was definitely not at home because she would never have allowed that. Sniffling and crying, I tucked my soggy tissue into her shroud, so she could have that bit of me to take with her; and, because she always liked to make sure she had a tissue in her pocket.

Then we buried her body. Because I am a shamanic practitioner I have a great respect for the concept of a "good death". This means one in which the person is given the freedom to leave without those left behind begging them to stay. As I had with my father, I let my mother go.

I am free now to love them, without fear they will not love me back, as with Dad. I am free now to be like them, to do the things they liked to do, to enjoy the things they enjoyed. My parents loved the opera, but I couldn't stand the sound blaring through the house while I tried to sleep as a child. Now, like as not, the classical music station is often on in my home, and I no longer rush to change the station when the opera comes on; rather, I feel my parents close to me in those moments. The dead never truly leave us. Their memories and words, hobbies, loves...these things have a way of percolating in our lives anew, sometimes bringing new insights about their lives, and sometimes enhancing our own lives. As William Faulkner penned, "The past is never dead. It's not even past."

"Go home. I want you to have a life," quoth Mom. That turned out to be harder to achieve than I'd imagined. Without my responsibilities for my mother as the map of my days, what was this life I was going to have? I couldn't write...a block crept in that was pure granite. Mom passed in August, and I spent an empty winter feeling bereft, and orphaned, and isolated. My son had recently been graduated from university and chose that time to move to California.

Grief support group helped.

And then, one day, as it always does, "April comes like an idiot, babbling and strewing flowers." (*Spring*, Edna St. Vincent Milllay). I threw myself body and soul into gardening, and yard work. I talked to my parents all the time, and gratefully, they didn't talk back. But I carried them—still carry them—in my heart, and my mind hears their voices reminding me to turn the clock back, or check the spark plug.

No, Mom isn't there when I want to call her and tell her about some recipe I just concocted, and there is no Dad to forget my birthday yet again. But I am connected to the memories, mostly good ones now, and I see them in the faces of my son and nieces. Moreover, I see myself more clearly in the continuum of our family. Now my siblings and I are the elders. During Mom's last hospitalization, the one right before hospice, when she refused to eat or drink anything anymore, I asked her something. "Mom, so what wisdom have you learned in all your 86 years? What is the most important thing in life?"

Without hesitation, in a firmer voice than I'd heard in weeks she said, "Family."

I tend to agree. Whether it is your birth family, your spiritual family, your work family, or your family of friends, it is the family of humanity that connects us all, that holds us in magnetic resonance of belonging and love.

We exist together in one big bottle of soap bubbles...beautiful, fragile, touching each other and wavering with delicacy and urgency, each one unique, each one shimmering; each one a vessel of infinite possibilities as we are blown through the magic wand of existence... Bouncing on the breeze, floating into the stratosphere, lighting the sky until the bubble bursts and leaves an incandescent imprint of what has come and gone.

PROSPERO:
Our revels now are ended. These our actors,
As I foretold you, were all spirits, and
Are melted into air, into thin air:
And like the baseless fabric of this vision,
The cloud-capp'd tow'rs, the gorgeous palaces,
The solemn temples, the great globe itself,
Yea, all which it inherit, shall dissolve,
And, like this insubstantial pageant faded,
Leave not a rack behind. We are such stuff
As dreams are made on; and our little life
Is rounded with a seep.

THE TEMPEST Act 4, scene 1

Caveat

For eons, grieving people have sought to connect with their loved ones who have passed on. Séances and Ouija boards are a few of the ways in which people have explored trying to communicate with those dearly departed. It is not at all unusual for the living to continue to feel their loved one's resonance for a time after a death or longer if there wasn't a successful transition. The dead may continue hanging around the living for a period of time, especially if they are implored not to leave even as they are trying to cross over. Of course they do not belong partly here. They can be gently guided home; however, assisting these suffering souls to reach the light, or trying to communicate with them can have destructive results for both the living and the suffering dead who have not fully crossed over. **DO NOT TRY THIS ON YOUR OWN.** This is serious work that must be facilitated by an individual who has proper training in how to intercede on behalf of the non- living in order to ensure the well -being of both the living and the departed.

Epilogue

It is called a *magic wand* for good reason. Go outside and breathe life into some bubbles....let the magic begin!

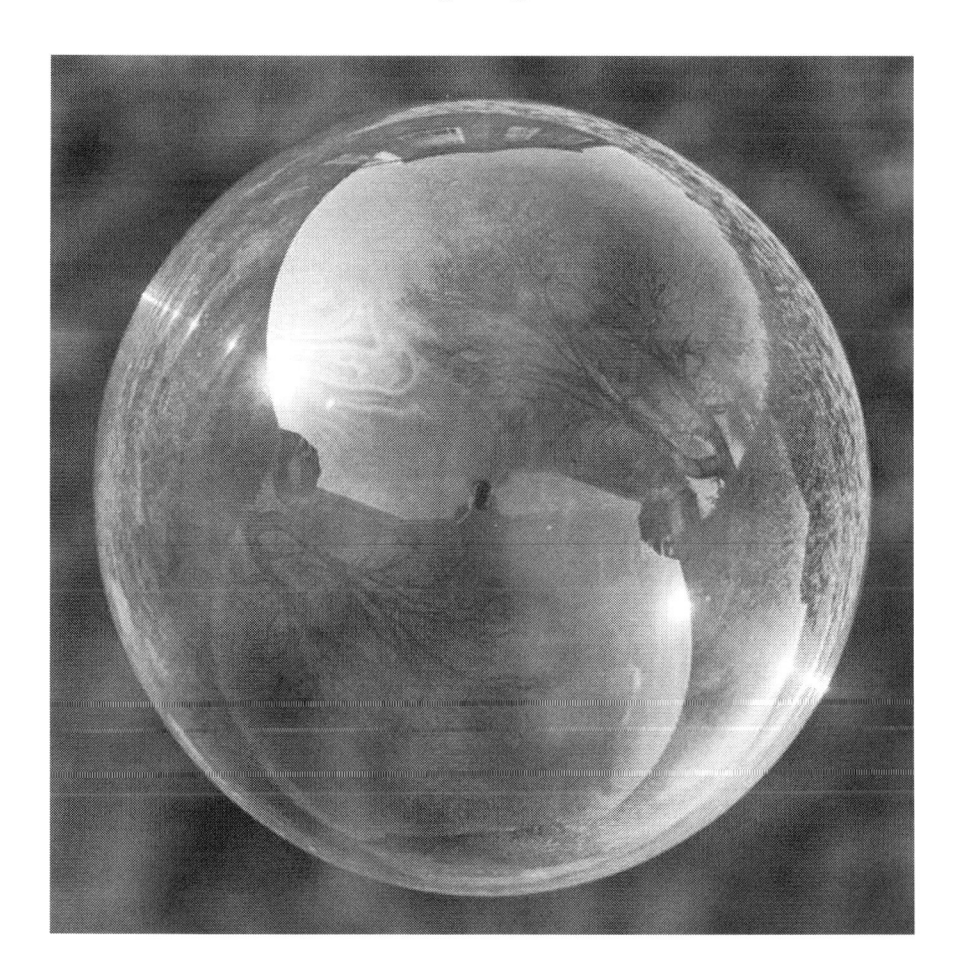

End Notes

For more information about Shamanism, Vision Quest, finding a teacher or healer:
www.shamanicteachers.com
Foundation For Shamanic Studies: www.shamanism.org
Society For Shamanic Practitioners: www.shamansociety.org
Dance of the Deer Foundation: www.shamanism.com
http://www.ewebtribe.com/StarSpiderDancing/wheel.html
http://www.whale.to/b/sunbear.html Sun Bear's vision
www.winddaughterwestwinds.com/Bear_Tribe_Med_soc.html

Meditation Resources:
www.shambala.com (Shambala Publications),
www.wisdompubs.org (Wisdom Publications), www.harpercollinscom,
WWW.LLEWELLYN.COM
www.soundstrue.com
Your local metaphysical book store.

Nature Resources:
National Park Service U.S. Department of Interior: http://www.nps.gov/findapark/index.htm
National Wildlife Federation
11100 Wildlife Center Dr. Reston, VA 20190-5360, www.nwf.org/
State Parks of the United States: www.stateparks.com/usa.html

Botanical gardens:
http://en.wikipedia.org/wiki/List_of_botanical_gardens_in the_United_States

Zoos in the United States:
en.wikipedia.org/wiki/List of zoos
http://www.arbreptiles.com/zoos.shtml

Shakespeare Festivals:
www.stratfordfestival.ca
www.shakespearefellowship.org/linksfestivals.htm
http://www.dmoz.org/Arts/Performing_Arts/Theatre/Shakespeare/Festivals/United_States/

Opportunities to Volunteer:
www.forgottenharvest.org
www.peacecorps.gov/
www.habitat.org Habitat for Humanity
http://www.americorps.gov/
www.mowaa.org Meals On Wheels
www.bbbs.org/ Big Brothers Big Sisters

Federation of Jewish Welfare Organizations
home.earthlink.net/.../federation_of_jewish_welfare_org.htm
www.nami.org National Alliance for the Mentally Ill
Your local church or temple, nursing home, public school, or social service agency.

Bibliography

Andrews, Ted, *Enchantment of the Faerie Realm*, Llewellyn Publications, 1996

Bach Flower Essences for the Family, Wigmore Publications Ltd., First Ed. 1993

Bear Heart, with Molly Larkin, *The Wind is My Mother, The Life and Teachings of a Native American Shaman*, Berkley Books, 1998

Bergstrom, Betsy. *"Heart Centered Depossession."* E. Lansing, Michigan. 18 Feb. 2005

Black Elk, Recorded & Edited by Joseph Epes Brown, *The Sacred Pipe, Black Elk's Account of the Seven Rites of the Oglala Sioux*, University Of Oklahoma Press, 1989

Bruchac, Joseph, *The Native American Sweat Lodge History and Legends*, The Crossing Press, 1993

Bugental, J.F.T., *The Search for Authenticity*, Holt, Rineheart & Winston, Inc., 1965

Cameron, Julia, *The Artist's Way, a Spiritual Path to Higher Creativity*, Tarher Putnam Books, 1992

Cole, Toby, *Acting, a Handbook of the Stanislavski Method*, Crown Publishers, 1955

Collins, Terah Kathryn, *The Western Guide to Feng Shui Room by Room*, Hay House, Inc. 1999

Cumming, Robert Denoon, Editor *The Philosophy of Jean-Paul Sartre*, Random House, 1965

De Saint Expury, Antoine, *The Little Prince*, Harcourt, Inc., 1943

Eshowsky, Myron. *"Peacemaking."* Leaven Center. Lyons, Michigan. 2 June 2002

Foster, Steven, with Little, Meredith, *The Book of the Vision Quest, Personal Transformation in the Wilderness,* Prentice Hall Press, 1988
Goldstein, Mark, *"Dharma Talks,"* 1980 -2012
Harner, Michael, *The Way of the Shaman,* Harper Collins, 3rd ed., 1990
Heeks, Richard, *Bubble Photo,* www.amazingdata.com/soap-bubbles
Hittleman, Richard, *Yoga, 28 Day Exercise Plan,* Bantam Books, 1969
Honervogt, Tanmaya, *The Power of Reiki, An Ancient Hands-on Healing Technique,* Gaia Books Ltd., 1998
Ingerman, Sandra, *Soul Retrieval, Mending the Fragmented Self,* Harper, 1991
_____, *Medicine For the Earth, How to Transform Personal and Environmental Toxins,* Three Rivers Press, 2000
_____, *"Healing With Spiritual Light,"* Kellogg Biological Station, Michigan, August, 2004
Krishnamurti, *Inward Revolution,* Shambala Publications, 1979, 2005
_____, *The Awakening of Intelligence,* Krishnamurti Foundation Trust, Ltd, 1973.
Luhrs, Janet, *The Simple Living Guide,* Broadway Books, 1997
Macrone, Michael, *Brush Up Your Shakespeare!* Harper Perennial, 1994
Mantegna, Joe, Et. al., *Bleacher Bums,* Samuel French, Inc., 1977
Merriam-Webster, Collegiate Dictionary, 10th Edition, Merriam-Webster, Inc., 1998
Secunda, Brant, *"Alaska, A Living Dream,"* Juneau, Alaska, Summer 1999
Shakespeare, William, *As You Like It,* Pocket Books, 1960
_____, *The Tragedy of Antony and Cleopatra,*
_____, *Sonnets,* Crown Publishers, Inc., MCMLXI
_____, *The Sonnets An Illustrated Edition,* Tiger Books International, 1993
_____, *The Works of William Shakespeare,* Universal Classics, Leon Amiel
Spolin, Viola, *Improvisation for The Theatre,* Northwestern University Press, 1983
St.Vincent Millay, Edna, *"Spring,* www.theotherpages.org/poems//millay01.html

Sun Bear, with Wind, Wabun and Mulligan, Crysalis, *Dancing With The Wheel, The Medicine Wheel Workbook*, Fireside, 1991

Sun Bear, Wind, Wabun and Shawnodese, *Dreaming With The Wheel, How to Interpret and Work with your Dreams using the Medicine Wheel*, Fireside, 1994

Tulku, Tarthang, *Kum Nye Relaxation*, Dharma Publishing, 1978.

Terebelo, Marc, D.C., Lecture, Farmington Hills, Michigan, 2006, 2008

Wahlstrom, Ralph, *The Tao Of Writing: Imagine, Create, Flow*, Adams Media, 2006

Winkler, Gershon, *Magic of the Ordinary, Recovering the Shamanic in Judaism*, North Atlantic Books, 2003

http://ypen.com/361/

www.enotes.com/shakespeare-quotes

www.nosweatshakespeare.com

www.sparknotes.com/shakespeare/hamlet/quotes.html

www.giga-von.com/quotes/authors/William_Shakespeare

http://www.mcsr.olemiss.edu/~egjbp/faulkner/quotes.html

About the Author

Frannie R. Goldstein is a shamanic practitioner, numerologist, Reiki master, Ceremonialist, teacher, mother, writer, gardener and student of the human condition. She maintains an occasional hand in acting and directing. She has authored poems, plays and short stories. She enjoys the four seasons of her native Michigan.

She can be reached by email at: followyourheart_2@msn.com

Printed in Great Britain
by Amazon